My chair

"… my chair is always in its place
My chair is the axis of the world,

is my eternal rock.

In this world, there are far too many empty
things.

Yet my chair,

even when unoccupied,

is not empty."

Kim Chong-mun (1919 - 1981)

Bibliografische Information der Deutschen
Nationalbibliothek:

Die Deutsche Nationalbibliothek verzeichnet diese
Publikation in der Deutschen Nationalbibliografie;
detailierte bibliografische Daten sind im Internet über
http://dnb.dnb.de abrufbar.

© 2024 Martin Schmidt-Magin

Verlag: BoD · Books on Demand GmbH, In de Tarpen 42,
22848 Norderstedt

Druck: Libri Plureos GmbH, Friedensallee 273,
22763 Hamburg

ISBN 978-3-7693-1477-9

Six days after the U.S. atomic bombings of Hiroshima and Nagasaki on August 6 and August 9, 1945, Emperor Hirohito announced the end of the 'Greater East Asia War' in his address on August 15. This marked the beginning of the end of the suffering endured by hundreds of thousands of young women and girls, who were exploited by the Japanese military as sex slaves, euphemistically referred to as 'comfort women,' during World War II.

On August 14, 1991, Grandmother Kim Kah-soon publicly acknowledged for the first time that she had been a sex slave of the Japanese military; since 2012, August 14 has been recognized as the 'International Memorial Day for Comfort Women.'

To date, over 100 memorials commemorating this crime have been established worldwide. In 2011, the bronze sculpture 'Statue of a Girl for Peace,' created by the artist couple Kim Seo-kyeong and Kim Un-seong, was unveiled in front of the Japanese Embassy in Seoul.

Several reproductions of the 'Statue of a Girl for Peace' stand — tolerated, but not necessarily welcomed —in various places around the world. One of these statues was displayed in August and September 2018 in the foyer of the Dorothee Sölle House in Hamburg-Altona, Germany.

Dr. Martin Schmidt-Magin shares his personal perspective on the 'Statue of a Girl for Peace' in the form of diary-like reflections on his encounters with activists."

To Nuna

Girl Statue for Peace

– Comfort Women –

– my personal journey

by
Martin Schmidt-Magin

REGARDEUR Xen

"I was a sex slave of Japanese military"

- Torn hair symbolizes the girl being snatched from her home by the Imperial Japanese Army.

- Tight fists represent the girl's firm resolve for a deliverance of justice.

- Bare and unsettled feet represent having been abandoned by the cold and unsympathetic world.

- Bird on the girl's shoulder symbolizes a bond between us and the deceased victims.

- Empty chair symbolizes survivors who are dying of old age without having yet witnessed justice.

- Shadow of the girl is that of an old grandma, symbolizing passage of time spent in silence.

- Butterfly in shadow represents hope that victims may resurrect one day to receive their apology.

Content

1.   Foreword   11

2.   Part 1   16

3.   Part 2
       Bonn / Germany   35

4.   Hamburg / Germany   40

5.   Korea   49

6.   Review and Outlook   99

7.   Appendix   102

8.   Epilog   108

9.   Images   119

       Impressum   3

Kintsukuroi is the traditional Japanese method of repairing earthenware, celadon or porcelain. The existing fragments of a vessel or object are glued with lacquer and missing pieces are added. These glued areas are not covered with paint but sprinkled with the finest gold dust. The broken vessel is restored to its original form, the scars are clearly visible, but the dignity of the vessel is preserved through the transformation of the repair.

Top: Example photo of Kintsukuroi
Right: 'Statue of a Girl for Peace,' bronze, stone, 2011, in the foyer of the Dorothee Sölle House, 2018

Foreword

"Mr. Martin! You are the artistic director of this project?" "Yes." "Then I have something to tell you, namely my impressions of this memorial. You see, like you, I am a man. And I have to tell you ... I cannot approach this statue. My own terrible experiences resonate too strongly within me at the sight of this young girl. I was also a victim of assault in my childhood and obviously I still haven't processed and resolved this old issue. My wife drew my attention to today's event and I went along with it, completely naive. And now, look at me. I'm standing here in the foyer of the Dorothee-Sölle-Haus, as far away from the statue as I can get and yet so close that I can just about see it. And inside? I'm shaking inside." "It is remarkable and speaks volumes for you that you are facing up to this experience. Another lady told me roughly the same thing just a few minutes ago. She also had to endure sexual assault in her youth and can look at the sculpture from a distance, but can't really approach it. And yet, she said: on a second visit, when she is alone with the sculpture here in the foyer, she will approach it and will certainly take a seat on the empty chair. Maybe that's an approach for you too."

This short sequence of conversations almost completely outlines the theme of the "Statue of a Girl for Peace": A memorial against sexual assault. A monument for the observance of human rights. A clear statement for "A NO is a NO!" A cry for help from all those girls and young women who were and still are abused, raped and killed in war zones as easy prey for marauding soldiers. She, the statue, "Pyeonghwabi", is a call to all of us: "Finally put an end to sexualized warfare! Finally put an end to violence against women!" Sexual abuse against weaker people has been happening for as long as people can remember. It is finally time for the male part of our society to become aware of its own responsibility and to recognize and internalize that intolerance and humiliation, degradation, violence and torture cannot be a means of dealing with the female sex. The bronze "Girl Statue for Peace" gives us, the viewers, the opportunity to get back in touch with our own inner child, who has been beaten and hurt by father and mother, friends and educators. And by making contact with the inner child, healing can take place for ourselves, through acceptance and forgiveness, as well as for others, because our own healing leads to compassion, respect and under-standing.

The "Girl Statue for Peace" was originally created in South Korea, explicitly as a memorial against the sexualized violence perpetrated by the Japanese military against girls and young women in the occupied territories in the Asia-Pacific region during the Second World War. Scientists assume a shockingly high number of victims and put the figure at between 200,000 and 400,000! And of course there are institutes and researchers who doubt these figures. But even if "only" 10,000 victims had suffered sexual violence at the hands of Japanese soldiers, that would be 10,000 victims too many! Every woman, every girl who has to suffer sexual assault is one victim too many! So the statue and its roots are firmly rooted in the conflict between Japan and Korea. However, the fact that we have transported a copy of the statue to Germany and erected it here within the scope of the German constitution gives it a much broader, general meaning. The statue becomes a universally understandable symbol that transcends borders and cultures.

In my personal experience, the individual and personal contact with the "Girl Statue for Peace" takes place in several stages. First, the sculpture is perceived from a distance, in its naturalistic form: a girl in unusual clothing is sitting on a chair, next to it is another chair, but unoccupied. On approaching closer, details of the statue become perceptible: the girl looks strangely impassive, staring ahead of her with empty eyes. Her hair is cut short, chin-length and unkempt, rather disheveled. Her hands are clenched into fists and pressed in front of her lap, her feet are not firmly planted on the ground but hover slightly above it. A small bird sits on her shoulder. Behind the girl on the plinth of the statue, a mosaic formed with black stones creates a shadow, but not of the young girl, but of an old woman, clearly bent forward and sitting with a hair bun on her neck. The shadow is mosaicked with broken black stones; in the center is a stone made of white marble in the shape of a butterfly. The bronze chair to the girl's right is empty. If the statue has already been captured so far, then the plaque attached to the statue can also be read, the text reads:

"This statue of a girl for peace commemorates the suffering of the so-called "comfort women" who were forcibly prostituted by the Japanese military government during the Second World War. Around 200,000 women from the occupied Asian countries were abducted to military brothels and sexually abused. The memorial commemorates the suffering of the victims of this inhumane war crime and makes a contribution to restoring the dignity and rights of the women affected. At the same time, it is an ongoing call for peace and serves as a symbol of remembrance for all people who are still victims of sexual violence around the world today.
In solidarity with all people in the world who are committed to peace!
August 14, 2018"

And at the latest now that the accompanying text has been read, the "V-effect" sets in, the stylistic device of epic theater initiated by Bert Brecht: the alienation effect. An action is interrupted in such a way that the audience's illusions are destroyed. The illusion that the "statue of a girl for peace" is one beautiful but insignificant sculpture among many is shattered. No, this high-quality statue is by no means trivial; it contains both explosives and healing. Explosive for those who seek violence and confrontation, healing for those who open themselves up to conversation and exchange, who can look at their own wounds and injuries and develop stability in the present and strength for the future by accepting their own roots and origins.

Grandmother Lee Yong-soo made me realize during my visit in November 2019 on the occasion of her 90th birthday in Korea that "Acknowledge - Forgive - Let it blossom!" - is the right formula for dealing with our own history, however terrible or beautiful it may have been. Only by facing up to our past, recognizing it for what it is and acknowledging that it is over, that we can regain strength for our present through forgiveness, that we can reflect on ourselves again and allow new and peaceful things to blossom in the future from these insights, only then can reconciliation happen and a work of art, a painting or a sculpture can also help.

Yes, it is possible and happens again and again that we literally "die" of awe before the concentrated power of a painting by a Leonardo da Vinci, a Rembrandt, a Picasso, a Damian Hirst; yes, that is possible. But: in front of the bronze sculpture "Girl Statue for Peace", we as viewers are reached on a completely different level. It is not the superficial level of veneration, but the level of personal-individual concern. We can recognize ourselves in the sculpture of the bronze girl; we can identify with her, merge with her and from this unity a new perspective can arise that helps us to understand that there need be no rivalry between men and women, that men can understand women and - as in Taoism - only the unity of Yin and Yang (female and male energy) can and will result in a unified strength! The "Girl Statue for Peace" gives courage and strength! In other words: "See it - Say it - Sort it!"

Part I

"I was born in clay from ore by fire...
    my sisters reside all over the world"

I was designed in the studio of the Korean artist
couple Kim Seo-kyung and Kim Un-seong in Seoul,
South Korea. My original mold, the model for the
marquette, the casting mold, was created in a loving
atmosphere based on respect and tolerance. I only
too gladly remember the warm and soft hands of
Seo-kyung and Un-seong, who initially poured liquid
plaster and later warm wax over my inner metal
skeleton, applied it and finally - as I said - smoothed
it out with their hands. In the top layer of wax, they
both modeled - very tenderly - my body, my skin
and the clothes I am allowed to wear, the hanbok,
the traditional garment of Korean women and the
fine fabric shoes. The model for the two, who have
no children of their own, was a young girl of around
13 years old from the studio's neighborhood. She is
one of the many children who, driven by curiosity,
press their noses against the large windows of the
studio hall again and again to catch a glimpse of the
interior. As Seo-kyung and Un-seong are only too
happy to see children playing around them, a small
fan base of neighborhood children has formed since
the two artists moved in, who drop by the studio
almost every day. They occasionally bring fruit or
sweets to the artists, sometimes they get up to
mischief by pressing the doorbell or knocking on the
huge gate and of course running away immediately
afterwards; but sometimes they also sit on the old
sofa in the studio in complete awe and watch the
process of creating drawings and sculptures with
their eyes wide open, often also with their mouths
wide open.
Seo-kyung and Un-seong liked one of the girls so
much that they asked her parents if Sumi, which is
her first name, could be the model for the bronze

sculpture "Girl Statue for Peace" that was to be created. Her parents were reluctant at first. They run a small grocery store in the nearby shopping center, right by the entrance leading to the bowling alley, where all the family's hands are needed to help, as none of the family of five can do without each other, as everyone is entrusted with a fixed part in the business. However, when Seo-kyung and Un-seong assured them that Sumi would only be a model for a few hours on a few days and that the times could of course be arranged together, the parents agreed. In the meantime, they had also spoken to many of their clients about this "project", as they called it, and learned that it is an honor when an artist asks to model for them.

What made Sumi stand out from all the other children in the "fan community" was her always friendly nature. No one could say that they had ever met Sumi in a bad mood or that she had not responded to a request for help. Sumi was a proverbial ray of sunshine for her family and all those who came into contact with her. During the many hours she spent at her parents' stand in the large hall of the shopping center, she was meticulous in making sure that whenever a person in need of help appeared at the glass door and did not immediately open the heavy doors themselves, she or one of her two brothers would rush to their aid. Her highest commandment to herself and her siblings was that they should always carry out this small service to others with a smile on their faces. Sumi was also known as the "Little Sun" by her competitors in the shopping center; everyone, really everyone, appreciated her friendly and pleasantly lively manner, which she sometimes even spiced up with a little joke or a bon mot to amuse the bystanders. Sumi literally brought light into the dreariness of the shopping center.

And yet little Sumi's parents wondered why the artist couple had chosen their child. For Sumi's parents, the little girl was more of a cheeky brat who occasionally took on too much and sometimes lacked the dignified and reserved respect for other people. In alcohol-fueled conversations, her father was even tempted to describe Sumi to his business partners as a disgrace to the family. However, those who knew Sumi's father knew that he and his daughter were one heart and one soul and that he would never have raised a hand against her, nor would he scold or berate her.

The parents' astonishment only emerged from the moment they learned about the content and theme of the "project". In their imagination, a sad girl, a girl severely scarred by life, perhaps even a disfigured young woman would have to take her place as the model for the "Girl Statue for Peace"; but they gladly complied and promised to support Sumi in her first modeling role.

I was created in the image of the lively Sumi. Her appearance is even, her origins from a family in the northeast of the country's capital and multi-million metropolis Seoul, which is more poor than rich, are not visible. The rather hard facial features of her great-grandparents, who lived between the Sarak-san Mountains and the Yellow Sea, and the soft physical appearance of her ancestors, who came from Jeju, the largest island in Korea, and found their new center of life in Seoul, the new capital of the Republic of Korea, after the Great Brother War; she combines both antipodes in herself and Sumi can truly be seen as a Korean beauty who harmoniously combines opposites and who can also be quickly identified as a Korean girl by Europeans and Americans. And although she was already 14 years old, her round, full face still radiated a lot of childishness, which was not only due to her slightly bulging cheeks.

I believe that my "parents" could not have made a better choice. However, the fate of the girls and women I symbolize is unimaginably harder, more horrible and disgustingly violent compared to Sumi's life. All the more I admire the choice of Seo-kyung and Un-seong, who also in this "project" let the small flame of respect, recognition and appreciation of those women who were so badly beaten by fate light up.

I myself learned quite late about the fate of those women for whom I was to symbolize in the future and for whom I now stand. The emergence of my raw form was, as I mentioned above, characterized by love and tenderness. However, the more I grew into my final form, the more clearly and distinctly I was able to perceive what was happening around me. While at first it was only feelings related to myself, pure perception and sensing of the relationship between artist and work, my senses became sharper and sharper and eventually I could not only see my surroundings but also hear what was being said around me.

I liked what I saw in the studio back then. The spacious and tall factory building, which just a few years ago housed a production facility for sanitary facilities, is now undergoing a transformation phase - you could even call it a slumber. Like an area-devouring cancer, the Seoul octopus is growing ever further into its own suburbs, incestuously absorbing everything that has grown in traditional slowness. It is destroying the small urban structures, razing them to the ground and forcing them out to make way for high-rise apartment buildings with up to 30 storeys; crammed into residential areas enclosed by fences, guarded at the entrances and exits, only accessible by car and sterile due to their modular construction. A description of the building's architecture would not help a visitor unfamiliar with the area to find the residential building. But the K+E factory building still defies demolition and offers a refuge for intellectual, cultural and political exchange.
When I first looked through the studio, I noticed a

composition of three framed prints by the German expressionist artist Käthe Kollwitz above the aforementioned sofa group; wonderfully expressive woodcuts that denounce the poverty and torment of the working class, the disenfranchised, women and children: framed and backed by the sentence: "Never again war!", a young woman can be seen, her hair disheveled, her clothes dissolved and her right hand stretched high into the air, like an exclamation mark she stands up for her demand. On another sheet, a young woman kneels in front of a corpse, holding her hands desperately in front of her face. The third print shows an obviously still young woman, visibly pregnant again, holding an infant in front of her chest and holding another sibling on her left. Her face is gaunt and sunken, deep circles have formed under her eyes. Her figure is bent; she has not been able to accuse and demand for a long time, fate has broken her.

On the same wall are drawings, woodcuts and posters by artists from the Korean Minjung movement, which was formed as a reaction to the Gwangju massacre in May 1980. At the time, South Korean dictator General Chun Doo-hwan ordered the brutal suppression of a student-led demonstration against the ruling military dictatorship and for democracy. Over 100 people were killed, over 4,000 injured and hundreds were considered missing after those days. The artists, including O Yun, Im Ok-sang, Kim Pong-jun and Hong Song-dam, used painting and woodblock prints in particular to express their call for democracy and the reunification of the two Koreas. Their criticism focused on imperialism, Americanism and the authoritarian South Korean government. The everyday struggle of the workers, nature, but also family and everyday life formed the focus of their artistic work and their world view. They conveyed clear messages in clear lines. Accordingly, the two sculptors want to see themselves as socially critical artists who do not get lost in an "art for art's sake" movement, but who

look closely at current social conditions, both in their home country and around the world, and who make their contribution with the products of their hands to the visualization of injustice, combined with a solution approach: art in the service of humanity!
In contrast to these propagandistic print products, which obviously denounce social conditions and injustices, are her sculptures and sketches, which are very inconspicuous and never demanding or aggressive; however, they are in no way inferior in terms of quality to the other artists mentioned or even have to hide behind them.
Because, even though I stand for an inconceivable crime against humanity, committed by Japanese men during the Second World War, I would have initially expected to present myself to the world in a fighting, or at least suffering, maltreated and with a threatening gesture and aggressive attitude. But the first glance in a mirror told me otherwise. Seo-kyung and Un-seong immediately translated Sumi's beauty and life-affirming world view into me. They placed me on a small wooden stool, dressed in the hanbok of young girls, but without the metal jewelry holding the dress together above the breasts, which often contained a small metal pin in an ornate sheath. Of course, this could have been used as a weapon against attackers or against myself. I hold my hands in my lap above my thighs, my fists clenched tightly. Both feet have no grip on the ground, the balls of my feet hover above the granite floor. Directly under the chair is a black spot in the shape of the shadow cast by an old woman sitting bent over. How do I recognize it? From the bent back and the hair bun on the back of her neck. This shadow is formed from individual shards of black marble; a mosaic of shards embedded in a white base of gray granite slabs. A white marble stone in the shape of a butterfly is embedded in the center and clearly visible. It lies flat and immobile, anchored to the ground.
Nevertheless, the butterfly symbolizes that transformation is possible! Its three-dimensional

counterpart can be found on my left shoulder, a little bird, perhaps a robin or a wren. And this also stands for positive change, for hope and new beginnings. And my gaze? It is directed inwards. No eye contact is possible here, I am completely closed off, withdrawn and no longer capable of any emotional movement.

To my right on the granite base plate is a second bronze stool, empty, unoccupied ... there's room for you here!

During the many weeks of designing and modeling my form, Seo-kyung and Un-seong kept me hidden from prying eyes. The only exceptions were the aforementioned neighborhood kids' fan club and, of course, Sumi herself. Artist friends, other colleagues or even gallery owners, activists or collectors were deliberately kept away from the studio during the time of my creation. Only when Seo-kyung and Un-seong were sure that they had found my final form in perfection were they prepared to show me to a small number of hand-picked personalities and contemporary witnesses, i.e. those affected. After all, who better to decide on the quality of a symbol than those grandmothers who have been raising their voices on Wednesdays for years, in Seoul's city center, in rain, snow or heat, in exhaust fumes and particulate matter? Numerous grandmothers, or halmonies in Korean, were invited to this first public viewing by the artists. The inner tension of the grandmothers dissolved into screams, lamentations and weeping at the sight of the statue, i.e. in front of me. Tears of emotion, anger and relief ran down the wrinkled cheeks of the elderly women. I can't remember how many hands touched and caressed me that evening. Each and every one of those present sought contact with me and sat down on the empty chair to pose for a photo, while the others crowded around me and behind me to find a place in one of the countless photos. Everyone's throats were full of praise and finally there was singing and dancing, the pent-up emotions found many forms of expression on this evening, which finally ended with a delicious dinner.

So the first hurdles were overcome. In the meantime, it was also decided that my place, my installation site, should be directly in front of the Japanese Embassy in Seoul at the site of the Wednesday demonstrations. The necessary funds for the production of the bronze cast and the stone base plate were collected and then it was time to check the effect on site with a specially produced plaster cast in original size. Covered in gold bronze and mounted on a handcart for easier transportation, I finally rolled this cast in front of the entrance to the Japanese Embassy.

The effect was impressive. Initially eyed with suspicion by the police who were standing by, the mood of the policemen changed to bright laughter on closer inspection. I had to put up with snide remarks, but some of the police officers supported our action and helped me to find a place on the sidewalk. But the mood quickly changed again when the policemen realized the effect of this seemingly simple action. The shouts of the demonstrators grew louder and with even stronger voices they chanted in chorus for justice, for recognition, for reparation. By grouping themselves around me, taking me into their midst and pointing at me. The weeping and pleading of the grandmothers became all the more urgent now that, with the help of my presence, a pictorial representation of the victims in their childish and youthful age had been added. Now it was no longer just old women who brought back images of the past with their words, but now everyone present could see with their own eyes that crimes were committed against children and young people during the Second World War. The atmosphere on this Wednesday afternoon became increasingly oppressive. Fortunately, the police allowed the demonstrators to continue their verbose and loud but non-violent actions that afternoon, retreating to the opposite curb in front of the Japanese Embassy and, in the absence of any current instructions, simply standing as a closed phalanx with the embassy building behind them. At nightfall, I was driven back to the artist's studio. Seo-kyung and Un-seong could now be sure that they had done exactly the right thing by creating me the way they had. The reactions of those affected and passers-by were clear: my journey could continue now that the first stage had been successfully completed.

Back in the studio, preparations began for my upcoming casting in bronze. Seo-kyung and Un-seong reworked the wax surface of my casting mold, the marquette, then they attached the channel system with the sprue funnel and the so-called wind pipes, the air escape channels, which were also made of wax. This procedure took a long time and eventually I found myself in a veritable ball of waxy ducts. In the next step, Seo-kyung and Un-seong coated me with a thick layer of molding sand, which they girded with several steel bands. The mold was finished. Several helpers had come to the studio the next morning to lift me onto the air-suspended flatbed of a truck and off we went to the foundry. With the help of a crane, the unloading process was faster than the loading. And then I found myself immersed in one of the bronze foundry's many casting pits. Just in time, because the tapping of the blast furnace, where the bronze ingots had been melting for hours, was now imminent. More clay was quickly placed between the casting mold and the pit wall and tamped down. Then the foundry workers put on their asbestos protective suits, put on their protective hoods and the big moment of casting was imminent. The foreman pushed open the opening of the blast furnace with a long rod, pushed the slag from the opening to the side and the stream of metal, at over 1,000 degrees Celsius, poured like lava into a channel that was aimed directly at the sprue of my mold. The heat now penetrating the mold immediately vaporized the wax with a great roar and hissing, the ground shook with the transformation I had just gone through, but a few seconds later silence returned. The work of the casters was done, that was all they could do. Whether the casting was successful or not would only become clear hours later, after the mold had been smashed; now we had to wait. In the late afternoon, the time had come. Auxiliary workers uncovered the mold, the familiar crane picked it up and set it down at ground level in the workshop. Using heavy sledgehammers, the workers removed the layer of clay, cut through the metal strips and the first glimpse of the raw casting made everyone present, but especially Seo-kyung and Un-seong, beam with joy. Yes, the casting was a success. Disk grinders were now used, with which skilled workers removed the casting tubes and my desired appearance became more and more visible step by step. In the days that followed, Seo-kyung and Un-seong could do nothing more than wait and trust that the skilled workers, chasers and patiners would carry out their work and deliver the best possible result. Those days were hard for me to bear. Compared to the tender modeling by Seo-kyung and Un-seong, the constant, deafening hammering and grinding of the metal surface by the chasers' tools was torture. Finally, the patineurs applied an acid mixture to the bronze surface using gas burners to achieve the desired yellow-gold color and complete the casting.

When I finally found myself in the showroom of the foundry, in a room lined with mirrors, next to a multitude of other bronze figures, I felt pride for the first time in the work my parents had done. I, a beautiful bronze statue, had come to life. I would now take my place as a representative of hundreds of thousands of young women and girls and stand solidly and firmly, even immovably, in one place as a symbol for them, for these victims. In just a few days, I would be standing in front of the Japanese Embassy building again. How much I was looking forward to it.

But first I wanted my parents to see me. And it wasn't long before Seo-kyung and Un-seong approached me, hesitantly, as if they didn't want to disturb or frighten me, and slowly guided their steps towards me. As soon as they entered the exhibition room, their eyes were fixed on me and the closer they got, the more their eyes filled with tears of joy and relief until they were standing right in front of me. They held hands tightly, alternately looking at me and at each other. Yes, I am their work, they created me. From a technical and craftsmanship point of view, I was complete, but at the same time unfinished, because the mission was only in the early stages, this journey was only about to begin.

My destiny was set: I would be placed in front of the Japanese Embassy building in Seoul. But more of my siblings were to emerge and find their way into the world. So what we had just experienced was the beginning of a long story about "Recognize - Forgive - Let Blossom".

My transportation to the installation site in Yulgok-ro 2-gil Street was like a procession. The foundry employees drove me from the outskirts of the city to the center of Seoul on an open trailer held by a few lashing straps. Although only a few people accompanied me for the first few kilometers, several cars soon followed our transport and formed a procession. We chose the route via the wide Seong-daero, which leads directly to Gyeongbokgung Palace, the former royal palace, past Gwang-hwamun, the palace's large main gate, via Sajik-ro and Jong-ro-gil streets. At the southern end of Seong-daero, a large crowd was already waiting for us; they surrounded me and accompanied me the remaining several hundred meters to my destination.

Arriving at the sidewalk opposite the Japanese embassy, what felt like hundreds of Koreans carried me down from the trailer onto the asphalt sidewalk with pure muscle power and straps. They placed me directly opposite the entrance to the brick-colored Japanese embassy building. Loud cries of women accompanied the line-up, the piercing "Aygo" and the chanted calls for human rights, justice and recognition penetrated the high-rise canyons of the Jongno-gu district. A good 2,000 demonstrators had gathered on this Wednesday, December 14, 2011, the day the 1,000th Wednesday Peace Demonstration took place in front of the Japanese embassy.

With my constellation, the participants in the Wednesday peace demonstrations had a new symbol with which they could identify their ideas and demands. One participant, it was really very cold that day, put her own woolen hat on my head and put her woolen scarf around my neck. I had arrived, my only task now was to stay put and make an impact through my presence alone: Acknowledge - Forgive - Allow to blossom.

Performing my task is not quite as easy as it might sound. Of course I stay there, I don't move from the spot. I am taken in, insulted, beaten, lovingly touched. Shoes lie at my feet again and again, I am given clothes to protect me from the wind and weather, I find flowers in my hands and around me on the plinth. Wednesday after Wednesday, demonstrators gather and unwaveringly shout their demands in the direction of the embassy. They unfurl banners, form groups and take countless photos. A military policeman who is now on duty around the clock to protect me, according to the official version, reprimands passers-by who dare to sit down next to me. He prevents contact. On the other side, to my left, activists have erected a tent large enough to accommodate six people. The tarpaulin is transparent, so that these volunteers can immediately recognize imminent threats during their daily work, which they do in several shifts, and pass them on via cell phone and internet and, in case of need or even emergency, ask for help and support. Unfortunately, this is a precautionary measure that is as important as it is absolutely necessary.

The already tense atmosphere between the two governments of South Korea and Japan has continued to escalate in recent weeks. Japan's Prime Minister Abe repeatedly and blatantly called for an end to any discussion on the subject of "comfort women"; in a revisionist approach to history, he denied that there had ever been any assaults by Japanese soldiers against Korean women. All those women who had "worked" in military brothels during the Second World War had done so voluntarily. Neither school textbooks nor history books should mention this aspect of the war. The grandmothers, who have been speaking out for a few years now and publicly reporting on their difficult fate, truly paint a completely different picture.

When I arrived at the Japanese Embassy, the Korean military police increased their presence in front of the building. Initially with a good twenty soldiers patrolling around the clock as sentries. Later, several team buses blocked the front of the building. Front to back, the buses stood opposite me, the exhaust fumes from the constantly running engines directed flexible pipes from the exhausts into the sewers.

Not much happened in the meantime, but four years later, in 2015, movers began to clear out the embassy building. The diplomats moved into the adjacent Twin Tree Tower in a very short space of time, largely unnoticed by the public. At first the building stood empty. I was now looking at a hollow shell, guarded by soldiers. Had I done my job or was this a clever move by Japan's diplomats, who wanted my presence to come to nothing? A few weeks later, heavy machinery, excavators and cranes rolled up and began demolishing the embassy building, which was erected in 1976. After the building was razed to the ground, the construction workers erected a white fence several meters high around the property. In the same year, the Japanese government officially applied for permission to erect a new building by submitting a development plan. Approval followed immediately, but to date no further work has been carried out on the derelict and desolate embassy site. So I am looking at military buses guarding a piece of land belonging to the Japanese government, which lies completely unused in the middle of Seoul's city center. Just as the embassy building represents the country of Japan, the small wasteland now represents the country of Japan and its government; I really like this analogy.

In November 2018, a German art historian came to see me. It was already late afternoon and the sun was just disappearing behind the horizon dotted with houses. I had already spotted him, Martin, from afar. His height and European appearance made him stand out from the crowd of visitors today. Finally, his searching gaze met mine. Both of Martin's companions, a Korean woman and a Korean man, had obviously led him to me in a roundabout way, as this was the only way to explain their visible relief when they saw me. The fact that a Westerner, a non-Korean, is seeking my company is quite extraordinary, so I was all the more excited to see his reactions. With a very alert and attentive gaze, Martin surveyed the surroundings, my position and the passers-by standing around. The activists' large tent seemed to bother him, because his first comment was: "The way we walked to Sumi, she was completely hidden behind that big tent. No wonder we couldn't see her at all from a distance!" He stood at my left side, leaned forward and placed his hand on mine. Now he looked at the police cars and the white construction fence at the level of my eyes. "That's a sad sight. And anyway, why isn't the statue on a proper pedestal? Like the many sculptures here in public spaces? Every sculpture has a pedestal and an inscription stating the name of the artist, the title and the year it was created; but there is nothing like that on Sumi. She sits flat on the sidewalk, pushed up against the curb. As if she had been put down and forgotten. And even worse, ..." he paused for a moment, "... in German there is the term "Bordsteinschwalbe", a euphemistic description of prostitutes who ply their trade outdoors, on the sidewalk. What a sad coincidence." Just as he was about to sit down on the chair next to me, the police guard stepped in and held him back. "Do not enter the monument!" was his clear instruction. This may be a protective measure for outsiders, but for me it meant rejecting the sympathy I was meant to feel. Fortunately, the police officer at the Wednesday demonstrations enjoys no respect and those present sit next to me, stand behind me and give me recognition and affection, which I really enjoy. Martin, however, had to accept the fact that he was only allowed to stand behind me or at my side. While his two companions took photos and documented this moment of encounter, Martin continued to look at his surroundings. Suddenly he laughed out loud and pointed out that they, all three of them, had already been in the immediate vicinity this morning. "Why don't you take a look? Isn't that the café over there where we started the day this morning? Of course it is. There's also this huge and colorful sculpture of an urban hippster with his computer in one hand and a cell phone in the other. I took a photo of this thing, don't you remember?" But yes, they both remembered and now had to laugh and realize that they had actually been very close to me hours before.

Shaking their heads, they left me, but not without bidding me a proper farewell. They promised to come and see me again tomorrow straight after breakfast. I could still hear their laughter in the distance as the three of them passed the café I mentioned.

Speaking of Germany. In addition to my sisters, who have already been placed here in South Korea in the cities of Suwon, Sokcho and Busan, one of my siblings also made the journey to Europe, to Germany, and another one also came to Germany via the USA. I would still like to share the story of my sister "Suri", even though I probably can't remember all the details. Our family has grown to such an extent that one or two stories may be misremembered or a little distorted; I apologize for this, as this information can be found in the many publications on my and our family history.

The story of my other sister "Rumi" will then be told by Martin, the "Artistic Director of the Girls' Statue for Peace in Germany Project".

My sister "Suri" was donated by a group of citizens from the city of Suwon. It was presented as a gift to the mayor of the German twin city of Freiburg on the occasion of his visit to South Korea. The Green politician was delighted to accept the gift and promised to set it up in Freiburg. On his return to Germany, however, the mayor found out what a can of worms he had stirred up by accepting the sculpture in his home country. As soon as the project became known to the public, a storm of indignation from the Japanese government broke out against the mayor, causing him to abandon his intention and subsequently reject and refuse to accept the gift. At this point, "Suri" was already on its way to Germany. Now, deprived of her mission and vacant, my sister soon eked out a dreary existence, crammed into a wooden crate in the warehouse of a German shipping company.

It wasn't until months later that "Suri's" constellation talks in Germany started moving again. Another group of active Koreans from Berlin had established contact with a retired businessman near Regensburg. There, in Wisent, is the Nepal-Himalaya Private Park, a large area that was originally a quarry. The owner accepted the gift and made a place available for "Suri" in his extensive park.

The transportation from Freiburg to Wisent went without complications, especially as no third parties, i.e. those who were not in direct contact with the project, were informed. The public, and therefore the press, was only kept up to date to the second via social media channels in South Korea. Once she arrived in Wisent, "Suri" was finally able to leave her wooden crate and travel the few hundred meters to her new destination on the outriggers of a forklift truck. And then she had taken her place, on a small hill with a view to the southwest.

For the official inauguration on March 8, around two hundred people made a long procession along the winding paths through the park to the site where the "girl statue" was erected. Most of them had traveled from Korea, from the city of Suwon. There were several speeches in Korean, and a group of musicians, a Pungmul dance and music group, had traveled there especially for the occasion. The guest of honor, however, was grandmother Ahn Jeon-soon. She, now in her 91st year, had not shied away from the hardships of the long journey and enhanced the already meaningful ceremony with her presence. In keeping with her age and so aptly symbolic, she took a seat on the empty bronze chair. Grandmother Ahn and "Suri" sat next to each other. She, the grandmother, the elderly victim, representing all those who were robbed, tortured and maltreated by the Japanese military, and "Suri", the girl, bronze symbol of injustice, forgiveness and shared flourishing. The group of musicians performed folk dances and songs as well as a shamanic initiation ceremony. Martin was also invited to speak on this festive day, and his brief contribution was met with polite applause. Due to the really cold March weather, the official ceremony on site and outside ended after just over an hour. In the evening, the guests came together again in the ballroom of a castle near Regensburg and the following hours were filled with a series of musical performances and thanksgiving speeches.

The atmosphere seemed relaxed and the participants were apparently satisfied, but this was only an outward appearance. A dispute had arisen between the initiators and the owner of the private park, Mr. H., concerning the two text panels, which - also according to my reading - were and are an integral part of the memorial. The plaques, one in Korean and one in German, contained information about the history and placement of the bronze. They clearly named the Japanese military as the perpetrators and the women of the Asia-Pacific region, hundreds of thousands of them, as victims. However, Mr. H. was apparently pressured by the Japanese government not to erect the sculpture; if he were to erect it, he would do so without the information panels. Mr. H., who had purchased this disused quarry with his own funds and furnished it with plants and handicraft objects and buildings from the Himalayas and Nepal, was keen to create a park that unites beauty and conveys harmony. With the "Girl Statue" sculpture, he had now invited a point of friction into his own park. According to the park owner, a sleight of hand, namely not installing the plaques, was intended to pacify the Japanese side, but this approach, which was not agreed with all sides and participants, caused a split in the Korean donor community. It created tension between those who supported the plaques and those who could do without them. This condemnation was already rippling through the palace hall, but I was unaware of it. Nevertheless, without a direct reference to the history and circumstances of its creation, the "Statue of a Girl for Peace" degenerates into a purely popular bronze group whose deeper meaning cannot be grasped by the viewer simply looking at it. The entire drama and the abominable misery to which we refer in our manifestation as a statue, which appears so innocent, must be mentioned in text form in the immediate vicinity, as is customary in South Korea.

Since the honorable inauguration, "Suri - The Girl Statue for Peace" has stood in the Nepal Himalayan Park in Wisent as a purposeless part of the park with no indication of its origin or purpose. In a conversation, I heard that the owner of the park even referred to "Suri" as a "war girl". He also said that if another location for the public installation was found in a German town or municipality, the sculpture could be removed there immediately.

Part II

"Rumi" (the third) arrives in Germany from the USA - from Martin's perspective

Bonn / Germany

The exhibition preparations for Angelina Androvic Gradisnik's solo show at the Frauenmuseum in Bonn had been completed and the press conference had just finished when Ms. Yi arrived, as arranged, in the entrance area of the museum waiting for me and the director of the museum, Ms. Marianne Pitzen. I had been talking to Ms. Yi, or Nuna, or "older sister" as I call her - we were born just two months apart, but according to Korean custom, she deserves this name - for some time on the subject of "comfort women", the euphemism for these violent sexual crimes committed by soldiers against young women and girls. But I couldn't think of anything that would be conducive to the realization of the project, the permanent erection of the bronze group "Statue of a Girl for Peace". But finally, while setting up the exhibition in the Women's Museum, the proverbial penny dropped. Where, if not in the Women's Museum, which was the first of these institutions to be founded 35 years ago by Ms. Pitzen in the former German capital? This is exactly where the statue belonged! So I suggested a meeting between Ms. Yi and Ms. Pitzen. And today they met in the foyer of the museum. As I was still busy with some of the organization for Ms Gradisnik's solo exhibition, I left them alone in the foyer. Nuna knew what she wanted and Ms. Pitzen, as I got to know her over the past two years, was open to new things, especially if it fitted in with her museum's mission and she was able to present an important and controversial topic to the public. After a good hour, I found two people in the foyer who had obviously found a common denominator. In fact, the tenor had been found: "Yes, we'll do it! We'll display the statue of the girl here in front of the museum!" We immediately walked the few steps to the inner courtyard, the parking lot area of the museum, and Ms. Pitzen indicated a corner for the future placement of the sculpture; coming from the street, on the right side of the parking lot, right in front of the house wall. A worthy place, Ms. Yi and I thought, and we could only confirm the suggestion. This was the foundation stone for the commitment of the Punggyeong Weltkulturen e.V. association to place the "girl statue" on permanent loan in the Bonn Women's Museum. And, it could have been so good, but to cut a long story short, the project failed miserably. However, like a phoenix rising from the ashes, it marked the beginning of the presentation of the statue of the girl in Germany. But more on that later.

Over the next few months, the board of Punggyeong World Cultures planned the logistical and contractual aspects for the installation of the sculpture. There was still plenty of time before the planned installation in Bonn on March 14, 2018, but it was still important to draw up a permanent loan agreement, find craftsmen to lay the foundations and a freight forwarder who would not only transport the load but also help with unloading and assembly. Nuna kept in touch with Ms. Pitzen, by phone, email and in person, driving from Frankfurt to Bonn to keep her informed about our current efforts and to hear the status in Bonn. Unfortunately, the disappointment on our side grew month by month.

In order to raise funds for the realization of the project, Ms. Pitzen had also asked the head of the cultural department of the city of Bonn for support. But this contact had a fatal effect on the project. In the midst of the preparations, the head of the cultural department informed Ms. Pitzen that the Japanese Consulate General in Bonn had intervened on a massive scale with him and his office. The aim of this intervention was a clear demand from the Japanese side to prevent the "Girl Statue for Peace" from being erected in Bonn in front of the Women's Museum. Unfortunately, I was never shown the e-mails, letters or minutes of the telephone conversations; I was only vaguely informed of "difficulties", which ultimately led to the original idea being completely changed.

What exactly happened in Bonn, who intervened and in what form, who visited whom and made demands, was not passed on. But it delayed the entire planning and, above all, the contract that was ready to be signed in Ms. Pitzen's office was not countersigned. Instead, we received no response to the questions and emails sent to the Women's Museum. Months later, a Japanese journalist informed me that over 300 emails and letters had been sent by Japanese citizens in Japan and living in Germany to the cultural officer of the city of Bonn and to Ms. Pitzen, all demanding that the installation of the statue of the girl be stopped. The contents of the e-mails and letters were also not made available to me.

As the date of the planned installation was slowly but surely approaching, Ms Yi developed the idea of an accompanying program. An exhibition of hand drawings and diary entries by a Filipino girl stolen by the Japanese occupying forces was to be held as a solo exhibition over several weeks to draw attention to the topic of sex slavery during the Second World War and serve as a basis for discussion for a symposium that was to take place on July 11, 2018 in the rooms of the Women's Museum. The speakers were Griselda Molemans (journalist, Holland), Mina Watanabe (Director of the "Comfort Women" Museum, Tokyo, Japan) and Phyllis Kim (Director, Korean American Forum of California, LA, USA). Three women who had already made a name for themselves internationally with their work and research on the issue of sex slavery.

The sculpture, which was donated to the Punggyeong World Cultures Association for installation in Germany, had been stored unused for several years, packed in boxes in the halls of a shipping company in Los Angeles, USA. Years earlier, the statue had arrived in Glendale (greater Los Angeles area) and was to find a place in the city's public space. But here, too, the Japanese government intervened and plunged the organizers, the KAFC and its director Phyllis Kim, into a legal dispute that dragged on for several years. The result of this futile dispute was that the case was dropped, but time, money and nerves were wasted in vain. The Korean-American initiators had won in court, but it was foreseeable that the Japanese government would start another legal dispute as soon as the next attempt was made to erect the "girl statue" in Glendale. That is why Phyllis Kim, in her capacity as director of KAFC, transferred this version of the "Girl Statue" to the German association Punggyeong Weltkulturen e.V.. The sculpture simply had to be transported to Europe. At one point in our planning for Bonn, we had to decide to send the freight on its way. The transportation via ship route from Los Angeles to Germany took an estimated three weeks. The closer we got to the unconfirmed date of the planned installation in Bonn, August 14, 2018, the tighter the schedule became. Finally, we had to make a decision and requested the crates, i.e. we gave the "Go!" for transportation. We envisioned loading and unloading the cargo at one of the major European ports with a connection to the Rhine, i.e. Rotterdam or Amsterdam, so that the "girl statue" would be shipped on to Bonn via the Rhine and thus travel by water to its destination. At the beginning of June, the container ship set sail from Los Angeles, with three of the hundreds of thousands of crates containing the individual parts of the "Girl Statue". This version of the sculpture was produced, stored and delivered in nine individual parts: six granite slabs for the base, with inscription plaque and the shadow mosaic, two empty bronze chairs and the bronze figure of the girl. In this form, the sculpture was delivered from Seoul across the ocean to the American west coast and now from L.A. to Germany.

And while the "girl statue" was on its way across the ocean and then the Atlantic, the omens in Bonn changed. The installation date was increasingly called into question by Ms. Pitzen's reluctant position. But we had given the go-ahead for the transport, the statue was on its way, but there was no longer a location for the statue.

And then the Women's Museum put its money where its mouth was. The association was informed that the idea of erecting a bronze sculpture as a reminder and warning on the subject of "sex slavery in wartime" would now be implemented with a completely different focus. A sponsor had been found, a bronze foundry in the Bonn area, for the realization of a new sculpture to be created and a competition would be announced for which models were to be submitted. Our artist couple would also be allowed to take part in the competition for the realization. This was the end of our efforts to erect the statue of the girl in Bonn in front of the Women's Museum; it would have been a worthy and fitting place.

At that moment I decided to call my friend Axel Richter, sculptor and artistic director of the Haus am Schüberg in Ammersbek (near Hamburg), in response to Nuna's urgent questions about what should happen next. A new chapter was thus opened.

Hamburg / Germany

Axel Richter and I have been friends for many years. It began in 2006 when I briefly stood in as interim manager for the Japanese painter Rin N., who lived in

Germany/Frankfurt, but found that this older gentleman, who did not speak German and therefore always came to our meetings with a translator, lived in his own world with his own ideas of what was possible and what was not possible in relation to the German art market. Axel Richter had organized the exhibition of his "Opus Magnus" for Rin N., the presentation of a thirty-five-metre-long painting entitled "The Rhine". It was to be shown in no smaller or worse a venue than Ratzeburg Cathedral. In the end, however, the artist was unable to complete the painting on the agreed collection date. At the same time, he was unable to admit his failure, he went into hiding, there was no communication between him and Axel Richter. I myself was only insufficiently informed at this point, as I had only been able to meet Mr. N. shortly before and finally I had Mr. Richter on the phone, who asked me: "What's going on in Frankfurt? Where is the artist? When can I pick up the work? I'm on pins and needles here!" To cut a long story short: Since Mr. N. could no longer be reached, the presentation was canceled. However, Axel Richter and I agreed that we would simply sit down together on my next visit to Hamburg to discuss the whole thing again in peace and get to know each other. This happened a few months later. As a result, we continue to work together successfully to this day. For example, at the "Peace of Art" symposium, in which artists from Egypt, Palestine, Israel and Germany spent several days together at the Kunsthaus am Schüberg in Ammersbek near Hamburg and created works of art, or on the jury of the KunstHaus am Schüberg, at the many exhibition openings in the

KunstHaus and in Hamburg's two city churches, St. Petri and St. Jakobi. And now the next project came our way: the "Girl Statue for Peace" - Pyeonghwaui.

"And you're sure it will work?" I asked Axel Richter incredulously over the phone. But he said yes and described his vision to me. In a few weeks' time, an art event would start in Hamburg-Altona, which would bring together several speakers on the topic of "Dorothee Sölle and the political night prayer", who would give their very personal impressions and messages to an audience during the evening hours in front of the Evangelical Academy building named after Dorothee Sölle. This was to take place on three consecutive evenings at the beginning of August 2018, combined with an art performance by Nikola Dicke. The plan for this event was for the artist to use high-luxury overhead projectors (equipment that we remember from our school days) to project drawings, created using a multi-layered scraping technique during the speeches, onto the façade of the Dorothee-Sölle-Haus; she called this technique light graffiti. In addition to the overhead projectors, Nikola Dicke set up a projector that played a pre-recorded video clip in a continuous loop. The underlying theme was "criticism of capitalism", "stop the insanity of arms exports", "one eats the other" and the "statue of a girl also found a place" in this clip.

However, before these three evening events were to take place, Axel Richter said that the statue of a girl could be set up in the foyer of the Sölle House. That would fit in with the theme, especially as he was currently in contact with the Frauenwerk der Nordkirche and Ms. T. there. The modalities still had to be clarified, including how long the sculpture could stand there, but it all looked quite good.

A few days later, the okay came from the Frauenwerk Altona and Axel asked me about the current location of the sculpture. I hadn't looked at the consignment note yet and hadn't paid much attention to the transportation route of the bronze group. The disappointment over the indirect rejection from Bonn, which manifested itself as "I won't say anything and will just wait and see", was still too deep and the hope that the project would continue soon was too low. But when I looked at the consignment note, I had to laugh: the port of landing was Hamburg. So the "girl statue" had already been sent from L.A. to Hamburg, too nice a coincidence. Then that's exactly how it should be. We decided to regard the failure of the loan in Bonn as a fact and to give the "girl statue" asylum in Hamburg for the time being.

Again, just a few days later, on August 13, Axel and I were able to set up the statue in the foyer of the Dorothee Sölle House. It fitted perfectly into this foyer and visitor reception area, and not only in both our opinions. At the same time, it greeted the many hundreds of visitors and employees of the house every day and still occupied the space for itself and its profound message: equal rights for men and women, no sexual assault against women, a no is a no and #metoo.

On the day of the opening, the Korean Vice Consul General Kim invited the participants to lunch in an upscale hotel restaurant in the city. The artist couple had flown in especially for the event, as had a delegation including Reverend Lee from the Korean city of Suwon. The vernissage took place in the late afternoon with short speeches and thanks to all supporters and helpers, and the Korean Vice Consul General was present.

Immediately after the opening words, an older German woman rushed up to me and insulted me fiercely. "How dare you..." she began a triad. At the same time, a very emotional gentleman was trying to talk to me, so I simply turned away from the lady and made it clear to the gentleman that I would listen to him. He immediately began: "Doctor! You are the artistic director of this project?" "Yes." "Then I have something to tell you, namely my impressions of this memorial. You see, like you, I am a man. And I have to tell you ... I cannot approach this statue. My own terrible experiences resonate too strongly within me at the sight of this young girl. In my childhood, I was also a victim of assault and obviously I still haven't processed and resolved this old issue. My wife drew my attention to today's event and I went along with it, completely naive. And now, look at me. I'm standing here in the foyer of the Dorothee-Sölle-Haus, as far away from the statue as I can get and yet so close that I can just about see it. And inside? I'm trembling inside." "It's remarkable and speaks volumes for you that you are facing up to this experience. Another lady told me roughly the same thing just a few minutes ago. She also had to endure sexual assault in her youth and can look at the sculpture from a distance, but can't really approach it. And yet, she said: on a second visit, when she is alone with the sculpture here in the foyer, she will approach it and will certainly take a seat on the empty chair. Maybe that's an approach for you too."

Axel Richter and I wrote a short press release in consultation with the board of the Punggyeong Association and the women's department of the Protestant Church, which was also sent to the Japanese Consulate General for information purposes the day before the opening and inauguration of the "Girl Statue". Knowing that the "Girl Statue" was a red rag for the Japanese government, we wanted to carry out our exhibition project with the utmost transparency. The ensuing actions on the part of the Japanese Consulate General and our reaction gave us no respite for weeks. The Japanese side flatly demanded that the presentation of the "girl statue" be stopped immediately, that the statue be taken down immediately and that no discussion be initiated on this topic, i.e. sex slavery during the Second World War. These demands, which were now also brought to the attention of the most senior leaders of the Evangelical Church of the North, startled some clergy and dignitaries. Fortunately, however, important people in the circle of the Oberkirchenrat recognized that our action was a peaceful, non-provocative and non-blame-pointing exhibition. In addition, the

Protestant church did not have to comply with requests and expectations from the Japanese government, as the presentation was taking place on the church's own premises. We therefore received protection from the higher ecclesiastical authorities and were able to continue with the exhibition. But the Japanese Consulate General did not let up, and finally the Consul General, Ms. Fumie Maruyama, invited us to a meeting at the Consulate General in Hamburg's city centre. A visit to a foreign embassy or consulate means leaving the scope of the German constitution. As a rule, you hand in your mobile phone in the entrance area. Your identity card may even be confiscated for the duration of your visit. Complete video surveillance and the recording of all conversations is often the standard. This puts you defencelessly in the hands of the "host". We decided not to accept the invitation, declined the date and location, but expressed our willingness to meet in a public place, for example in the café of the Hotel Vier Jahreszeiten. This meeting did take place, although Axel Richter and I, the two artistic directors, were excluded as discussion partners, as the Consul General only wanted to talk to women, not men. So the head of the Frauenwerk Hamburg, who had come all the way from Lübeck, and Ms. T. appeared for the short morning meeting. Axel and I waited in the hotel's neighboring bistro café, within earshot, so to speak, just in case. After a quarter of an hour the spook was over, we were both informed shortly afterwards that the Consul General had started with small talk, but then moved on to the important points for her: stop the exhibition, dismantle the statue, no discussion on the subject of sex slavery. She then left the hotel. De facto, this "conversation" had brought no new insights, given no new impetus and evoked no new strategies for action.

It was clear to us that we would leave the "girl statue" in the foyer of the Dorothee-Sölle-Haus until the end of the planned exhibition and would not have to change anything.

At midday before the first evening of the campaign: "Dorothee Sölle - Political Evening Prayer", Axel and I had the idea, as we were driving to Altona together, to have a short video clip made by a cameraman and university lecturer in film and television who was a friend of Axel's. He was actually "only" supposed to document the "Sölle Evenings", but as he was present and had some free time before the first assignment, we thought he could simply point the camera at the statue. He was actually "only" supposed to document the "Sölle Evenings", but since he was there and still had some free time before the first assignment, we thought he could just hold the camera up to the statue and I could tell him a bit about the project. No sooner said than done. Off the cuff, we created a seven-minute clip, which was published on a YouTube channel shortly after filming. Within three weeks, this short clip had 14,400 views! As we found out afterwards, it was the Korean community that caused this little viewing sensation.

After six weeks, we dismantled the sculpture and moved it to a secure outdoor storage facility. At the end of the exhibition, we also removed the clip from the Internet.

We were able to present the "Girl Statue for Peace" to thousands of visitors in the Dorothee-Sölle-Haus in Altona, Germany, without causing a great deal of noise or offense in public. The reactions of those who saw the sculpture were consistently positive, discussions were stimulated and personal steps towards action and growth were initiated. The highest management level of the Protestant church, senior church councillors and the bishop were also informed and took a position within the church, either verbally or in writing. With the installation of the "Girl Statue" in the Dorothee-Sölle-Haus in Hamburg-Altona, all those involved had created a positive basis for further presentations of the sculpture in Germany. The discussion about abuse in the church that broke out at the same time also showed how topical the subject we had chosen was using the example of the "Girl Statue".

Nevertheless, the tactic of small pinpricks by direct and indirect representatives of the Japanese government must be pointed out. Unexpectedly and unannounced, but always with urgency, people repeatedly appeared at the site of the installation. Before hand, they sought exchange and conversation, but ultimately the aim was to influence and obstruct the project of erecting and presenting the "girl statue" in line with Japan's historical revisionist view and with the clear aim of preventing further erection. In order to achieve the explicit goals of the Japanese government - keeping the issue quiet, disregarding the victims, denying any responsibility - many people in Hamburg, just as in Bonn before, were set to seek contact with those involved in the project, to involve them in long conversations or to write and send long emails and letters, manipulating the opinions of those contacted in the direction of the Japanese government's thinking. Often, people who were only marginally involved were contacted and, in the form of "Whatsabout-ism", pseudo connections and non-existent connections were pointed out, which on closer inspection turned out to be obsolete and completely constructed, but which somehow felt logical at the moment of the personal conversation, so that the people contacted could not immediately object. These conversations often led to the seemingly trivial questions: "Do you know where the sculpture is now?", "Do you know what the next steps are?" or: "Who actually owns this statue?"

Korea

Duwon, Korean businessman for cosmetics in Germany, board member of Punggyeong Weltkulturen e.V. and one of its most active members, and Nuna picked me up at my front door. The journey to Frankfurt airport was uninterrupted. After a short stop at one of the airport restaurants, we were able to check in, went through security and waited only briefly for boarding. The flight on an ASIANA Airline A380 was comfortable and entertaining, even though we had booked economy. After a good eleven hours of flying, we landed almost on time at the international hub airport in Inchon.

We were picked up by Pastor Lee and a friend of Nuna's from university. Curious, I took in all the impressions that presented themselves to me. First of all, the modern airport, which I had last entered in 2003, shortly after it opened. The encounter with Nuna's friend was particularly funny, she looked at me again and again in disbelief, occasionally turning her head away and muttering: "So young, so young". The following hour-long drive to Suwon flew by. First over the thirty-kilometer-long bridge that connects Yeongjongdo Island with the mainland. Then the highway to Suwon, past a myriad of high-rise apartment buildings.

Our first stop was for lunch, and I had my first traditional Korean meal at a sports complex just outside the city. This was the start of a seemingly endless series of delicious restaurant visits. In my opinion, Korean cuisine is so varied and tasty that I found it easy to enjoy every meal, whether in an exquisite restaurant or a simple, rustic one. Much to the delight of my hosts. At this point I was very easy to please, I had - contrary to my vegetarian lifestyle at home - issued the motto: "I eat everything except dog meat!" On my previous visits to Korea, my first wife Helena's relatives had repeatedly pointed out restaurants whose specialty was dog meat. And, as is customary among family members, they also tried to take me to such a restaurant. However, as I understand the Korean language a little and can read a few words, I was always able to protect myself from such visits, and this time was no exception.

Nuna, who had planned the entire trip, had chosen the Vella Suite as the first hotel, very close to the birthplace of the artist Rha Hye-seok, Lee Ung-no's widow. A modern hotel with pleasant comfort and enough floors to meet my request for a room on the upper floors, at least from the fifth floor upwards. I was particularly taken with the rosemary tea offered for free tasting at reception. It was the first time I had seen the turntables embedded in the floor, which made it possible to maneuver the cars in a particularly confined space.

Pastor Lee and Nuna´s friend had taken the whole day off to accompany us in their city. The first excursion took us through the city center near a Buddhist temple. After passing a traditional imperial complex, the Hwaseong Palace, we visited the city's Museum of Contemporary Art. The large concrete block of the I´Park Suwon City Museum houses highlights from the hand of Rha Hye-seok. The presentation of her oil paintings featured a variation I had never seen before: Quotes by the artist were written on the exhibition walls in mirror image; they could only be read correctly by looking into the assigned large-format mirror surfaces. In my opinion, this was a very clever puzzle game that could inspire people to think differently or simply to think differently.

A pleasant view over the city, the Buddhist temple and the surrounding area awaited us on the roof terrace. We used the marked "best view points" to take what felt like countless photos, and they would not be the last.

A longer walk took us to the privately run Buddhist temple. The exercise and slight exertion on the climb up to Sungshinsa Shrine was really good after the long flight and car journey. Once we arrived at the complex, we were greeted by the sight of the ten-metre-high, fully gilded Buddha figure standing on a lotus blossom and backed by a mandorla. A few steps led down into the sanctuary, decorated with many swastikas and around one thousand two hundred small Buddha figures, lined up behind large glass panes. After taking off our shoes, we spent some time sitting in front of the shrine for inner contemplation and peace.

But we had obviously arrived at the temple very late, too late. The owners gave us a clear look and told us that visiting hours were over and that we had to leave now. The sliding doors to the sanctuary were closed directly behind us, but we were still able to visit the nearby pagoda with its bronze bell. The bell was a replica of a Korean national shrine, the Emilie Bell, actually: The Holy Bell of King Seondok. The original from the Bongdeoksa temple is in the National Museum in Gyeongju and was cast in 771 AD. According to legend, the bronze casters were only able to successfully cast the bell with the help of a shamanistic ritual; the ritual required a human sacrifice and a young girl was thrown into the glowing bronze. Many people still believe they can hear the heart-rending cry of the dying girl when the bell is struck. Young women who are abused by men to achieve their own goals; the main theme of our journey is fast approaching.

In front of the one-storey pagoda, a maple tree glowed in a blaze of red leaves; Indian summer had arrived in Korea and this wonderful play of colors in nature would now be our safe companion for the following days.

A short drive later, we found ourselves in the old town of Suwon. A meeting in the form of a dinner with the chairwoman of "Nabi", the Peace Butterfly Movement, was on the agenda. We reached a spacious, traditional restaurant via a quiet side street. In a separate room, a varied menu had already been laid out on low tables. We took a seat on the floor with our legs crossed. Bap (rice), guk (soup), kimchi, fish and other delicious side dishes, such as acorn puree, mung beans and finally home-pickled hanguk-bae (persimmon fruit); delicious!

Communication was somewhat difficult and bumpy for the first time at this meeting. The few bits of Korean that I was familiar with only helped me through the first few minutes of conversation. But after those present realized that the stranger, the "long-nose", could name one thing and another, but did not have enough confidence in his own ability to use English as an aid to hold a conversation, there was only one way out: to have the conversation with Nuna, with Ms. Yi. This was certainly effective and excellent, as she was the only person who had a complete overview of the "Girls' Tables for Peace" project and our trip. As a result, I was out of focus and could concentrate on the food.

As I had made it very clear in the run-up to the dinner that I would not be drinking any alcohol, not even mekchu, i.e. beer, the male guests were slightly displeased. Obviously, they had to abstain from alcohol - although this is traditionally part of the meal - if the guest does not want alcohol. So this dinner was under a slight time pressure and indeed, quite quickly - faster than expected anyway - and I know that Koreans can eat very quickly - the meal was ended with the hint that another meeting (this time probably with alcohol) was still to come, that we had to say goodbye now, but of course we had to take a photo together first; the proof of the meeting still had to be captured.

I encountered an endearing Korean peculiarity even before the photo shoot: the need to present the guest with a gift, no matter what the object is, only the gesture counts and is indispensable. So I suddenly found myself holding a three-footed mug made of glazed earthenware. One of our hosts had taken this special cup from one of the display shelves in the ceramic ginseng store attached to the restaurant and pressed it into my hand. At first I was at a loss as to what to do with this cup, especially as it seemed fragile to me; however, I now use it almost every day, it sits well in my hand and is very pleasant to drink from.

The day ended with a tour of the rebuilt and almost completely restored city fortress, which was arranged at short notice. Ms. Park was called especially for this and arrived on time for the photo shoot. It was then emphasized several times that a short, approximately fifteen-minute tour would now follow, which would give us an insight into the Suwon Fortress. However, the enthusiasm of our cityscape guide was so great that she led us over and through the historic city wall for a good forty-five minutes, giving us insights and views of a fascinating structure with outstanding gates, bridges and defensive walls. As night had fallen, we experienced the tour by floodlight, which further emphasized the grandeur and uniqueness of the complex. Visibly impressed, we were driven back to our hotel. That evening, I decided not to go for another, final evening walk, as I was now feeling too tired and jetlagged. The next morning revealed the full extent of my tiredness. I started the day quite crumpled, packed my suitcase and was looking forward to a classic Korean breakfast of bap (rice), guk (soup) and kimchi. Nuna had a similar idea and we went to the restaurant next door, which is open twenty-four hours a day, seven days a week and offers pork specialties. A deliciously hot and spicy morning soup helped me get the day off to a good start.

Immediately afterwards, we were picked up by Nuna´s friend Mi-gang and the day trip, which was under the aspect of Lee Ung-no, began. We drove to Daejeon. At this point, I would like to briefly mention that the Korean artist Lee Ung-no was one of the first interfaces between Ms. Yi and me. Back in 2017, we sat in Nuna´s office and talked about possible projects. As if in passing - and it was probably only in passing - she put a book on the table that was dedicated to the life and work of Master Lee´s work. I was immediately taken by the pictures of the exquisite paintings and asked for further details of his life. When I learned that there was a close biographical relationship between Lee and the Federal Republic of Germany, my interest was piqued. I had already dedicated a book in my REGARDEUR series to the bridge-builders between Korea and Germany: Li Mirok, Yun Isang and Franz Eckert. And now I recognized parallels to the life of Lee Ung-no. Born in Korea, he dedicated his life to art. After the fratricidal war, he saw no possibility for himself and his family to continue living in Korea. He left his homeland with a heavy heart and, with the help of the German ambassador at the time, left the country for Europe. His destination was the capital of Western art: Paris. But his first stop was in Germany, in Frankfurt/Main and in Bonn, the German capital at the time. There is a photograph from this period showing Lee standing with his son on the banks of the Main, with the Eiserne Steg and the Drei-König-Kirche in the background. In Frankfurt, there were also sales exhibitions of his prints and drawings in the Café KoZ (communication center) of the Goethe

University Frankfurt, which was run independently by students, and in the commercial Prestel Gallery.

In our discussions, the idea was quickly born to repeat the exhibitions in the anniversary year of 2019 and thus draw attention to this special artist, a pioneer and designer of figurative Informel, in two German cities. However, the research and discussions in both cities proved difficult and not conducive, so this project was shelved at the beginning of 2018 as still unsolvable. A trip to Korea at the end of 2018 gave rise to new hope. Once we had arrived in South Korea, we were able to spend time visiting relevant sites relating to Lee Ung-no's life and work. This was also the case on the second day of our trip. The drive from the hotel to Daejeon, 100 kilometers away, took a good hour and a half. Mi-gnan, who drove and accompanied us today, is a writer and musician, she organizes festivals and sets poems to music with her enchanting voice. We listened to some of them while driving through the vast and flat landscape of central Korea, which took us to two places close to each other. One was the historic birthplace of the artist, built in the traditional style, and its neighboring modern and functional staff museum. It was not possible to enter the birthplace, so the architecture merely served as a backdrop for the unimaginable photos. Nevertheless, sitting on the veranda created a physical closeness to the artist that the cold concrete walls of the modern museum building did not allow. In this place, the fusion of old and new architecture created a harmonizing unity.

The museum itself offered an extremely interesting selection of the most diverse works by Lee Ung-no from different phases of his career in 5 excellently lit rooms, in glass showcases and in front of exposed concrete walls. A place really worth seeing, dedicated as a personal museum to the life and work of an important artist of calligraphic "swarm painting". Wandering through the museum, the inclined visitor recognizes the high potential of stimulating energy that the artist brought to the West in himself and in his works.

In addition, what seemed impossible just a few years ago, artistic works by his second wife, Rha Hye-seok, were shown in the same house and actually mixed together in the same rooms. With this unusual presentation of the works of an artist couple, the curator proves how tolerant and open the Korean art scene is in recognizing the fruitful interaction between artists.

We decided to forgo a refreshing hot drink, which was served in the adjoining museum café, and drove the few kilometers to the Sundeoksa temple. We had a light lunch in an upstream parking lot and then set off on foot into the elongated temple complex. The destination and focal point of this visit was Lee Ung-nós home and place of work, which is located at mid-altitude. The artist had lived there for several years in monastic seclusion in a traditionally simple house. The house and adjoining utility rooms have been preserved in his honor and are now occupied by the monks who live there. In addition, however, a visitor center was built, which serves as a sales gallery for handicraft objects, contains toilets and other utility rooms, but also provides information on the life and work of the artist. However, the site also harbors a truly serious curiosity. During the many years he lived here in the temple district, the artist actually engraved Korean texts and, of course, his "swarm figures" into several granite boulders. These modern petroglyphs are carved up to 4 centimetres into the hard granite; a Sisyphean task when you consider that he only worked with a hammer and chisel and did not use any technical support in the form of compressed air or an electric angle grinder. When I put my fingers into the grooves carved out of the stone, I thought I could feel the enormous effort of strength and will of the artist in his time-consuming and energy-sapping realization.

In awe of the artistic and technical achievement, we walked up two more levels within the temple complex. Once we reached the top - but without even coming close to the uppermost part of the complex - our short touristy climb was rewarded by a Buddha figure laughing with both ears, several pagodas and a Kuanin figure, the goddess of mercy. We drank from a spring flowing into a granite basin with the help of the many plastic ladles provided.

The descent to the parking lot level had to be quicker, as the temple's closing time was approaching alarmingly, and there was also a light drizzle. Only now, on the way back, did I notice the many restaurants and stalls selling food and alcohol, handicrafts, many types of vegetables and, of course, ginseng in various forms - as a root, one, two or three-year-old, dried or preserved in alcohol, as a paste or powder. Unimpressed and without pulling out our wallets, we walked past the many vendors, including the sweet seller rattling his oversized metal scissors, who should have brought back childhood memories for Nuna and Mi- gnan, but obviously did not.

The drive in the dark to the nearest big city and the main train station was again entertaining and filled with conversations in two languages, music from the radio and lots of laughter. We had to go straight into the city center, which meant that we had to fight our way through the dense evening rush hour traffic. We only caught our train to Daegu by the skin of our teeth. But once we had taken our reserved seats, the pressure we had just felt in the car was gone. After just over an hour, we arrived at Daegu Central Station. Once again, we were greeted by a good friend of Nuna's. Professor Lee, a former fellow student, did us the honor of picking us up, taking us to dinner and finally accompanying us to our hotel.

The traditional meal we were invited to was exceptional. Abalone, Korea's special seafood, was served in a variety of ways: raw, steamed, fried and as a soup. Each and every one of these presentations was a culinary temptation; I hadn't felt hungry for a long time, but the exquisite taste and curiosity about the next palate-pleaser suppressed the feeling of fullness. The amazing thing about Korean cuisine is that you never feel full. No matter how much you eat, after a short while the obviously easily digestible food is metabolized.

It turned out that Professor Lee was not only a fellow student, but also a professor emeritus of the city's largest university and continued to lead the university's fortunes as a contact professor; he was also an avid forest hiker and a passionate seeker and finder of wild ginseng. We grabbed a cup of coffee in a small, European-style café nearby and were even taken to the hotel where we were to spend the next two nights. Finding the hotel wasn't quite so easy after all. But after getting competent help - at a police station - Professor Lee found the hotel, which was located in the old apothecary district of the city. Here, too, I was able to move into a room on the upper floors, with a view of various high-rise buildings and several streets. While zapping through the sixty or so TV channels on offer, eighty percent of which were Korean channels, I found a TV shopping channel offering the abalone shells we had just eaten for sale. These special mussels looked much more appetizing in the restaurant than on the screen in the hotel.

The next morning we were to meet Grandmother Lee Yong-soo at the HEEUM Museum - The Museum of Military Sexual Slavery by Japan - a first planned highlight of our trip, and in the evening we were to take part in the festivities in honor of her ninetieth birthday.

At first I wanted to skip the hotel breakfast, but my curiosity for something new made me go down to the second floor. I took the stairs and found out that the Korean cleaning staff used the stairwell to store their cleaning utensils and as a laundry room. With a few courageous jumps over small piles of hotel laundry, I reached the breakfast room. It was quite small and manageable. My expectation of white bread, butter and jam was not fulfilled, instead I was greeted by rice, soup, various types of kimchi and a few more side dishes; purely Korean. I took a small amount of everything and found a free seat on a stool in front of a window with a view of the street.

I have to make one more point about the toilets. In the first hotel, the day before, I was confronted with a fully electric toilet seat in the bathroom. The basic use of a toilet poses no challenges. From my previous stays in Korea, I was used to traditional squat toilets (as I knew them from France) or, on my last visit, toilet seats padded with foam with an opening at the front (American style), which took some getting used to even then. But now I was confronted with a toilet with a remote control. And in the first hotel, there were only Korean characters on it, no pictograms. I didn't want to get involved in "try and fail", so the translation help on the Internet had to clear up my predicament; to finish it off, I found the right buttons on this combination toilet of water closet and bidet.

Nuna, who was staying with an aunt nearby, found me sitting in the foyer, already carrying an umbrella.

Yesterday's rain had continued into the early morning and even now it was drizzling, so the sky was cloudy and gray in gray, the streets damp. She led me purposefully through the streets of Daegu's old city center. I tried to memorize the details. At first, I memorized the route, but when we both realized that the path we had taken did not lead us to our destination, we had to ask passers-by and finally reached the HEEUM Museum on a zigzag path, I kept an eye out for street objects that I could remember. In my case, these were the silhouettes of the high-rise buildings, especially their roof constructions, which were specific and individual when viewed from any angle, but also - appropriately for me - the large-scale sculptures that adorned almost every major building as "art in architecture". These point-de-vues were real anchor points for my orientation, which helped me later when I made my way to the hotel on my own; they were necessary and absolutely helpful.

Finally, a little damp, we reached the museum. We only had to wait a short time in the friendly but very dark foyer. We were registered and Halmoni, Grandmother Lee, interrupted an internal meeting with the museum's volunteers and director to welcome us. I don't know what made me think this, but I expected to see a frail, bitter old woman, perhaps in a wheelchair. Grandmother Lee Yong-soo was the mirror image of the opposite. Vital and wide-awake, she sat behind a large conference table in the museum's small office and scrutinized the two of us who entered. We were led to the table and sat down opposite Halmoni. Nuna took over the talking, and although I was able to speak a few words of Hangul, much to the delight and amusement of those present, I could neither follow nor participate in the content. So the exchange was interrupted again and again to keep me up to date with short, summarizing translations. We were informed about the creation and function of the museum and about Lee Yong-soo's personal journey. From her indescribably courageous action: "Now I'm talking!" to her stylization as the figurehead of the so-called "comfort women" movement in Korea. Stylization because sometimes all the hype about events that happened far in the past was too much for her. She does not want to be and remain stuck in the past. It is important to Grandma Lee to talk about forgiveness, reconciliation and the blossoming of a new togetherness and to live this shared blossoming. It was only at this moment that I realized that one of the volunteers was a native Japanese. And the visit of another Japanese couple, who also volunteered to support the museum, was announced at the same moment. Here in the museum, through the person of Halmoni, "reconciliation and commonality of Korea and Japan" is already being lived. This first conversation with the purpose of getting to know each other ended abruptly with the handover of Halmoni´s book from the "Remember Her" series, which she personally dedicated to me. The reason given was the arrival of the previously announced Japanese couple; I thought I sensed a trace of fatigue or restlessness in Ms. Lee. We, Nuna and I, were asked to take a guided tour of the museum.

Since visiting the museum was one of the main points of our trip, we gladly accepted the tour. I assumed that I would not see Halmoni again until tomorrow evening, at the public celebration of her ninetieth birthday, but I was wrong.

The museum, which commemorates the acts of sex slavery committed by Japanese soldiers, offers a variety of documents, facts and figures on two floors; presented in large-format photographs, in films that are shown in endless loops and in charts and tables. Several books on the subject and many merchandising items are on sale. The atmosphere of the museum fluctuates between darkly depressed about the terrible fate of the victims of the young women and girls forced into sex slavery by the Japanese military during the Japanese occupation to the hopeful blossoming of a vision of forgiveness and reconciliation that has already been partially realized. However, the demand for recognition by the Japanese government of the terrible acts committed by Japanese soldiers is also a top priority for the museum and its initiators, as is the demand for an official apology and reparation. The HEEUM museum, as small as it is, is definitely a beacon in the debate on how to deal with sexualized violence during the war. Unfortunately, all the information was only available in Korean; at least a translation into English would be desirable for the future in order to achieve a broader public impact. But this raises the question: Which tourists, which foreigners will find their way to the old pharmacy district of the city of Daegu? At least a bilingual presentation is essential for cooperation with international museums.

At the same time as the tour ended, we were told to get ready for lunch together. Not that I was hungry yet, but the hope of being able to experience Halmoni a little more made these concerns fade away. So we, a small, mixed group of Koreans, Japanese and me, a European, walked to a nearby Japanese restaurant, passing at least seven Korean-run restaurants; but no, it had to be a Japanese restaurant: Grandma Lee is already living the reconciliation of the two peoples that she claimed! I didn't really hear any of the table talk. Nuna was busy and carried out her role as representative and chairwoman of the German Punggyeong Association with dignity and intensity. I, on the other hand, concentrated on the sashimi and udon soup. Halmoni sat directly opposite me and I could see that her mood was lifting more and more. She talked a lot and laughed heartily again and again.

Lunch was followed by a short visit to the museum. There was an instant photo box in the foyer; we stood together on a marker on the floor, pressed the shutter release, all "Kimchi" and the photo was ready, the proof that captured the current visit. A total of three photos were produced and distributed in this way.

From the little information that was translated, I learned that Halmoni wanted to leave the museum and visit a hairdresser in the nearby shopping center. The idea of sitting with several women in a shopping center and then also at a hairdresser's made me feel uncomfortable and I decided to separate myself from the group and go back to the hotel to rest for a while. Nuna could only accept my decision, albeit disappointed. I was still standing with everyone at the entrance to the museum. When the cab arrived, I helped Halmoni in, said goodbye and walked down the street, waving, which I hoped would take me to the hotel. I found out later that Grandma Lee was not happy with my decision.

The sculptures I remembered actually helped me to find my way back to the hotel. I was able to return the umbrella, the rain had stopped and the thick cloud cover was breaking up more and more. Once in my room, I tried to sort out the impressions of the morning. The emotional shock that I had felt during my visit to the museum and when confronted with the documents of wartime shame dissipated more and more through my contact with Grandmother Lee. A woman who had to endure terrible things in her youth, who, despite suffering this martyrdom, was able to find her way back to a self-determined life after the war, a woman who confidently went her own way without the support of a husband, who finally stood up and showed herself, as a victim with her wounds and encouraged others to do the same, who put herself in the front row and undaunted and unabashedly and peacefully called again and again for recognition, apology and reconciliation, one can only pay the greatest respect to such a woman! Deep in these thoughts, the landline phone of the hotel room suddenly rang and Nuna asked me to come to the entrance immediately, because Halmoni insisted on going to a traditional teahouse with me. Since all my plans on this trip were externally determined, it was easy to follow this request. A traditional teahouse promised further variety and tea enjoyment, it was probably just around the corner, I would be served by service staff in traditional Han-buk and would be able to enjoy excellent Korean tea sitting in front of low tables on the floor; that was my idea. But things turned out differently.

Nuna was already waiting for me impatiently in the foyer. She told me that Grandma Lee didn't appreciate me leaving the group. Now she wanted to invite us both to a teahouse. She was also trying to reach her foster daughter so that she could join us. During the cab ride, I sat in the back seat next to Grandma Lee. She skillfully used her smartphone and talked to her foster daughter on the phone. She repeatedly showed me a photo of B., a beautiful young woman. The drive to the teahouse turned out to be a journey of just over an hour, as we drove from the center of Daegu out to the outskirts of the city. When we arrived at our destination, I found myself in front of a four-storey warehouse, the entrance was inconspicuous and when we arrived on the second floor and looked through the door into the interior of the floor, I looked into a spacious storage room filled with shelves, tables and seating furniture. And everywhere, really everywhere, were utensils for the use and enjoyment of tea: countless tea bowls, teapots, coasters, fireplaces, tea containers; in clay, metal, porcelain. An overwhelming number, a wealth of shapes and colors. Some of the exhibits were protected under glass lintels. The highlight of the collection was a Japanese tea bowl made using the Raku technique around 1927, deliberately destroyed during the Second World War, which was repaired in the late 1990s using the Kintsukuroi technique.

To my surprise - I had expected a low, small table and to be seated on the floor - we were shown to a large, full-height wooden table and seated on conventional chairs. The tabletop was decorated with several teapots, a few small tea bowls, cut flowers in a vase, a temperature-controlled kettle and edible snacks, such as a boiled sweet potato. A lady began to pour boiling water into small pots and hand us tea to taste. After the second or third round, she was replaced by the owner of the house, tea master Lee. The appearance of tea master Lee is completely unpretentious, in a gray jogging suit and a lived nonchalance, he casually celebrates the Chinese way of tea ceremony par excellence. Every move was perfect, the sequence of different teas was precisely choreographed and their subtle nuances of flavor precisely coordinated. This ceremony lasted almost three hours and was interspersed with a highly intellectual conversation about tea, people and existence itself. A pleasure through and through.

And we, the participants, Grandma Lee, her foster daughter, Nuna and I, enjoyed the afternoon. In Grandma Lee's case, this joy manifested itself in the carefree way she took me in her stride. She never left my side the entire time. She sought me out and repeatedly took my hand, much to the (feigned) horror of her foster daughter: "But Halmoni, you don't do that!" - "Yes, I do. I'm old, I can do that!" was Grandma Lee´s reply. Finally, there was a photo session, then dinner together in a nearby restaurant, but that would be too much to say. It was more like a kitchen in a garage. The cook was welcoming and the food served was extremely tasty: soup, kimchi and lots of side dishes. We dined at a round table with joy and appetite. Nuna finally took me back to the hotel in a cab and drove on to her aunt's house. Tomorrow would probably hold more surprises, I speculated as I fell into my hotel bed, completely exhausted.

I skipped breakfast in the morning, two full hot meals a day were enough and the hotel buffet wasn't that inviting after all. Nuna's friend was to accompany and chauffeur us throughout the day. The first item on the agenda was a visit to Daegu University. A few years ago, a sculpture was erected on this public university campus to commemorate the suffering of the "comfort women". It would be the first bronze sculpture on our topic that I was allowed to see in Korea. I was expecting a short visit, but once again I was way off the mark. Prof. Lee was already waiting for us in the visitors' parking lot. I was very happy to see him again, I had a very pleasant exchange with him the day before yesterday. We got into his car and he drove us around his former campus. Former, as he retired a few months ago, but the tributes from former colleagues and students showed how present

Professor Lee still was in people's minds today. It was really necessary to take the car, the campus of Daeju University with classroom buildings, dormitories, sports fields and many green areas was exceptionally spacious and also very beautifully situated. Finally, we arrived at the canteen and cafeteria. There, in front of the entrance area, she was placed, the other "girl statue" In gold-colored bronze, she sits on a simple metal bench, backed by a large-format poster, with a text panel at her feet. This statue of a girl, created in 2018 by Seo Yong-jun and largely financed by the student body, is much more naturalistic in form and more animated in its surface than that of the artist couple Kim. She sits forlornly on the bench, slightly bent forward, dressed in a han-bok, her long hair braided into a tight plait at the back, her bare feet hovering above the ground, her hands resting in her lap and holding a flower head. The students have become accustomed to the sight of the bronze statue, no one stops or sits down next to her on the cold bench, no shoes are placed next to her, no hand-knitted garments lie on the bronze's shoulders. We're the only ones who are looking at the statue, the hustle and bustle flows around this "statue of a girl for peace".

I enjoy the normality that prevails around the statue. It is part of this place, this square, it is part of it, without any great fuss and yet in and with its simple presence it reminds us of the suffering of the people for whom and for whom it is symbolically sitting here. Several photos later and after a heartfelt moment of silence, we went to the nearby cafeteria, where we took a short break with coffee and sweet pastries. I was allowed to order a specialty, a cold brew coffee. Ice-cold water dripped through the finely ground coffee grounds for a good twelve hours, this concentrate, which is characterized by the fact that there are no bitter substances or heated oils in it, was filled up with hot water in a coffee paper cup by the service staff. Finally, Professor Lee handed out some commemorative gifts and treated us to lunch at a restaurant very close to the university campus. A very special fish formed the centerpiece of this lunch, along with various types of kimchi, rice in a seaweed net and rice with reddish beans in a stone pot, slightly burnt at the bottom. Hot water is poured into this stone pot, causing the rice to separate from the bottom; the result is a slightly sweet, tasty drink.

After a warm farewell, Nuna's friend drove us to the Buddhist temple complex of Jikjisa. We parked the car at the lowest plateau and walked to the main complex, the path adorned with countless colorful lampignons, we walked through gates, over bridges, past tombs. Unfortunately, we didn't have enough time to walk further up, we were only able to take a tour of the temple buildings with the bell house, the Buddha hall, many pagodas and fountains, as well as outbuildings due to time constraints. The central square was also decorated with countless lampignons at head height, with a note attached to each balloon with wishes for healing, recovery and happiness for the writers themselves and for others.

The colors of Indian summer shone in the leaves of the many treetops and offered a beautiful, never-ending natural spectacle. I had never seen such a colorful backdrop before.

And we continued by car back to the city center of Daegu. Despite the onset of evening traffic, we reached the hotel without being pressed for time. A cab took us to Halmoni's anniversary celebration at the 5-star Prince Hotel. The ballroom was already well filled, with an estimated three hundred people having already arrived. Although we were registered, the people in charge did not immediately find our names in the entrance area, but one of the volunteers from the HEEUM Museum recognized us and clarified the situation. We were then let into the room and led to a table in the back row. We were just about to sit down to watch the goings-on from a safe distance when B., Grandma Lee's foster daughter, caught sight of us. She grabbed me by the hand and pulled me forward to Halmoni, resistance futile. With the heartfelt words: "Look who's come after all!" she pushed me towards her foster mother. Fortunately for me, Nuna was in my immediate vicinity, even if she didn't always do what I asked her to. When Halmoni saw me, she overturned the seating arrangement she had so well planned and asked Nuna and me to sit in the front row at her table of honor. I could feel the looks of the organizers at my back, they did not agree with this manoeuvre, but I complied with the 90-year-old's request, as I would do several more times that evening. In any case, Halmoni greeted us overjoyed, took me by the hand again and again and urged me to stay close to her. I stayed close to Halmoni for as long as I thought it was appropriate and then withdrew again and took a seat at the table, which was now occupied by various dignitaries. Each of the guests greeted the honoree and everyone wanted to capture the moment with at least one photo, so the first hour of the evening consisted of greetings and photos. Halmoni repeatedly wanted my presence at her side. She searched for me with her eyes and beckoned me to join her in the photos. The second part of the evening was led by a presenter. She obviously had a lot of fun announcing the individual program items, creating transitions, taking care of the technology that didn't always work and reciting prepared texts from various groups and people. I couldn't understand anything, didn't even try, but applauded and laughed along with the crowd; I was the only "long-nose", the only Westerner, in the huge hall. At one point in the evening, Nuna mentioned that all the important people had now been mentioned and that the buffet was about to open. This remark prompted the gentleman on my left to rise and leave the table without further ado. When he returned a short time later, he sat down, visibly satisfied, and told me in a few words of English that he had resolved the situation. Still surprised and wondering what he meant, I heard my first name echoing over the loudspeakers and "Dogire", meaning Germany. Seconds later, I had a microphone in my hand and was pushed forward towards the stage by my neighbor. Nuna grabbed a second microphone and instructed me: "Now it's your turn! Talk about our project, thank Grandma and send her congratulations!" I stood there in front of a good 400 guests and tried to start with a joke: "You can tell from my appearance alone, dear guests, that I am probably the only foreigner in this room. And indeed, my companion, Mrs. Yi, the chairwoman of the Punggyeong World Cultures Association and I have not shied away from the distance of a good eleven thousand kilometers and are here in Daegu today, on the occasion of the 90th anniversary of Grandmother Lee Yong-soo." While Nuna translated, I was able to sort out my thoughts. I then talked about how I had already thought about what to expect in Korea and in what condition I would see Grandmother Lee. I had expected a frail old woman and was so pleasantly surprised when I was introduced to a lively and energetic lady. I mentioned that we had erected the Girl Statue for Peace for six weeks in Hamburg the previous month and were making further plans to erect it in Germany. I ended this short speech with my best wishes to Halmoni and couldn't resist adding a little joke at the end. I concluded with: "Now I really hope that my partner, Ms. Yi, has translated the content of my words better than I pronounced them!" I was able to leave the podium to the uplifting laughter of those present. Shortly afterwards, the buffet was opened. This was followed by further musical congratulations and short performances. I felt that I had "done enough" that evening and made it clear to Nuna that I wanted to leave now. But her answer was clear: the timing was not right, we were the first and it wasn't appropriate. Although the rows of tables had already cleared a little, I complied, not knowing what to expect. Obviously professional stage actors entered the stage. The only words they spoke in English were: "Close the doors! There is no escape!" And then they got going, performing a potpourri of old hits, much to Halmoni's delight. Many of the songs had guests jumping up euphorically and performing dance interludes. Halmoni's eyes met mine again and again, she asked me to dance along, and if she didn't ask me, one of the guests did. I stood next to her for almost the entire duration of the song interlude and danced alongside her, with her or solo. Whenever I wanted to retreat, there was already a dear guest who asked me to get up and dance again. From my previous trips to Korea, I knew how much Koreans enjoy singing and dancing, so I was actually prepared and ended up enjoying this special evening. So much so, in fact, that at one point I took the initiative. When a song with the rhythm of a disco fox came on, I asked B. to join in and led her through the song, making her dance all kinds of turns and figures. When the song ended, she settled down exhausted, but one of the professional dancers grabbed me at that moment and thought she had found a passable dancer in me. To her great disappointment, I didn't understand her dance steps and as she wouldn't let me lead, we stumbled more than we danced. Halmoni, however, enjoyed herself, sang several times and danced again and again. Finally, the ninety-year-old had to sit down and rest; the evening was drawing to a close. Even the last dance enthusiasts had come to their senses and the presenter declared the party over. The hall quickly emptied and I found myself standing alone in the foyer. Nuna was busy, as was the foster daughter. I couldn't find my way into the hotel on my own, so I stood and waited. Suddenly Professor R. came looking for me. During the evening, I had observed several times how almost every guest, after paying their respects to Halmoni, went to him in order to be noticed by him. The professor, however, made no attempt to approach anyone in the room. But now he stood next to me, accompanied by his wife, and started a conversation in English: "So, you're from Germany!" A fluent conversation ensued and business cards were exchanged; I could feel the surprised looks on the faces of many of the guests still present. After a few fulfilling minutes, we said our goodbyes, the professor and his wife left the hotel and I also noticed that Nuna had said goodbye to all the important people and we were about to leave. A quick hug to say goodbye to Halmoni, the handing over of a host gift and the foster daughter did not miss the opportunity to accompany us personally to the cab. Dressed in the traditional Han-bok, she stood by the roadside until we lost sight of her.

Nuna confirmed to me that we had made good use of the opportunity to position our cause and that we were perceived by the guests as representatives of the Punggyeong World Cultures Association in Germany, which is intensively committed to the interests of the "comfort women".

The next morning we took the KXT train very early to travel from Daegu to Suwon. An official meeting with the mayor of the city was planned. We were to meet Rev. Lee and Duwon from Frankfurt again. Rev. Lee and his Peace Butterfly Movement in Suwon is undisputedly one of the main initiators of the "Girl Statue for Peace" project, without his unwavering commitment "our" sculpture would not have made it to Germany.

He picked us up at the train station and took us to the city hall, there was not enough time to visit the "Girl Statue" in the city park opposite before the meeting, this had to wait until after lunch. We were greeted by a full team of secretaries at the council and town hall, even though it was a Saturday. When I imagine a town hall in Germany on a Saturday, I see closed doors and empty rooms. In Korea, many things are different. When we entered the office area of the Vice Mayor of Suwon City, everyone present immediately jumped up, turned towards us and greeted us with a slight forward bend of the upper body. They remained upright until we had disappeared into the next room. There, in the deputy mayor's anteroom, wide and very comfortable leather armchairs offered a further welcome. Unfortunately, I didn't know the other participants personally, nor did I know the deputy mayor, so I expected every new person entering the room to jump up as well. The anteroom was filling up noticeably, after all there were ten of us, a lively conversation had already started, business cards were exchanged when Duwon arrived from Frankfurt; he had brought us to the airport in

Frankfurt six days ago, now he was here in Suwon to support our joint project.

Our conversation with the Vice Mayor was intended to highlight the ongoing initiative of Germans and Koreans living in Germany. We also wanted to ask whether there was a way to give us, the delegation sitting in front of the vice mayor, a mandate to take care of the relocation of the sculpture in Wisent; out of a private park, which can only be entered every six months and for an entrance fee, and into a public park in a major German city. When we entered the spacious room of the deputy mayor and I noticed the large round table, which could easily seat fourteen people, I whispered to Nuna that I agreed with everything she had done. I asked her not to give me time-consuming translations of the individual speeches but, if at all, only brief summaries of key passages, especially those of the deputy mayor. She could bring my position, which she knows almost word for word, into the discussion without consultation. However, if I were to be addressed directly, I would ask for a translation. During the hour that followed, there was an intensive and attentive exchange of ideas, Nuna neither found the time, nor did it seem necessary to include me in the conversation or translate content for me. So I sat in this group, looked at the participants, wondered about the large rail network map lying in front of the deputy mayor and followed the calm discussion with polite attention, without understanding a single word. At one point I sensed a caesura, obviously the different positions had been exchanged, but the mood was such that no decision had been made that immediate action would now follow. At this moment, I took the floor and spoke again in a short summary speech about the international significance of the issue of sex slavery in war. I explained how important the placement of the statue of the girl in Germany was and how helpful the sculpture was in the fundamental discussion about respecting human rights, equal rights for men and women, the topic of "A NO is a NO" and the #metoo movement. I had the feeling that the Vice Mayor was listening with interest to what I was saying, and I thought I could see on his face that I was both expanding on the comfort women issue and directing his perception beyond the bilateral Korea-Japan issue to the global significance of the issue. This, I thought, gave the seemingly small sculpture a presence and weight of content that it had not previously had for the deputy mayor. His closing words were very friendly and warm, which led to the obligatory photo opportunity and exchange of gifts. Unfortunately, this meeting ended without the handover of a concrete mandate for action for our delegation. We were invited to a nearby restaurant for lunch. There we sat together at a long table in a separee, the deputy mayor asked me to sit opposite him. I had Nuna at my side, so we were at least able to exchange some small talk about my work as an art historian in general and my work as Director of Art for the girls' statue project at the Punggyeong Association.

Afterwards, Duwon, Pastor Lee, Nuna and I took the opportunity to visit the sculpture of the girl statue in the city park opposite the town hall. This city park, the size of a soccer field with lots of green space, had room for several sculptures. The statue of the girl was therefore not a prominent monument, but one of many in this park. Overall, the high frequency of statues and monuments in Korea is striking, quite comparable to the monument inflation in the German Empire between 1871 and 1914. Art in architecture and sculptures in public spaces are omnipresent in Korea today, so this is not a special feature in the land of the morning calm.

From the town hall, all we had to do was cross the road, three lanes in each direction, and a sign would point us in the direction of the statue. The small city park was beautifully laid out, with gently winding paths that criss-crossed the park and met at several intersections to form small, open squares. The green areas were planted with bushes and shrubs, naturally with glowing yellow gingko, red maple and green pines. Just a few steps from the road, we found the "Girl Statue for Peace". The bronze statue is mounted on a large granite pedestal divided into eight segments. As always, she is sitting calmly and serenely on her bronze chair, with the empty bronze chair next to her and a plaque at her feet to the right and left. Further information on the history, creation and interpretation of the symbols used in the sculpture is provided on a large wooden plaque close by. Although this plaque is placed very close to the statue, it is so far away, respectfully, that it does not obstruct or even disturb the calm overall view of the statue. This Saturday, girls' shoes, soft white ballerinas, were found next to the statue's feet as a sign of support and sympathy, placed there as a gift from passers-by who are aware of the importance of the monument. As if to provide shade for the statue, a large pine tree stands next to the statue, like a guardian over its well-being. The "Girl Statue for Peace" was given a truly honorable installation here in the city of Suwon. Rev. Lee´s joy at the overall situation and our recognition of his efforts was clearly visible in his beaming face. Filled with pride, he allowed himself to be photographed in front of and with the "girl" and also asked us again and again to pose for photos with him and the statue.

Duwon, who was obviously visiting the city of Suwon for the first time, showed his enthusiasm, which grew more and more when we briefly told him about the magnificently restored city wall, which we had been able to walk along at night two days earlier. His curiosity was immediately aroused and he separated from our tour group to spend the next few hours walking the historic city wall that surrounds the city center. Pastor Lee told us to get into his car as quickly as possible, he knew that the traffic was getting heavier and he knew that our onward journey to Seoul would probably take longer than initially planned. It would be desirable to arrive at our meeting point for the afternoon at least roughly on time, especially as four people would be waiting for us there.

As predicted, the traffic got heavier and heavier. Our destination was the National Museum of Modern and

Contemporary Art (MMCA), which was opened in 1986 in Gwacheon, a southern suburb of Seoul. I was familiar with this museum from a previous trip, so I was all the more excited to see a familiar place again; but I was even more excited to meet the artist couple again: Kim Seo-kyung and Um-seong. They both wanted to wait for us at the museum and drive us to our hotel in downtown Seoul after a tour. I had admired Nuna's organizational skills from the very beginning; she actually managed to organize several people in such a way that we were practically passed from one hand to the next. Each of the people involved in this tour de corée gave me the feeling that they were happy and interested in this tourist and driving service; they not only made an effort to choose the places to visit, but also carefully selected the restaurants and food, endured the adversities of traffic and, as far as their mutual language skills allowed, sought to exchange ideas.

Whether or not we arrived at the Museum of Contemporary Art on time or late was not for me to judge. However, I was surprised to see that a huge leisure park with an integrated zoo had been established around the extensive grounds; neither the zoo nor the leisure park were there on my first visit. The immense size of the park meant that both driving the last few kilometers and finding a parking space became a major problem. We then arranged a meeting point near the artist couple's car via cell phone with all the people involved. This meant that Nuna and I could reload our bulky suitcases and Pastor Lee didn't have to waste any more time looking for a parking space in a traffic jam. The greeting with the artist couple, a former school friend of Nuna's, Mr. Park and the daughter of Nuna's friend U. was just as warm as the farewell to Pastor Lee. The daughter, I., turned out to be a real stroke of luck for me. She studied biology at the renowned EWHA Womans University in Seoul and spoke English that I could easily understand, she was interested in art and had the time and inclination to accompany us that weekend. So Nuna was relieved of the burden of interpreting, she was able to devote herself to her areas of interest and I found myself in the company of a student who was happy to show off and expand her English skills.

The Museum of Modern and Contemporary Art had a big surprise in store for me and was also to be a highlight of this visit. The architectural center, i.e. the hub of the huge museum complex, was the staircase - based on the New York Guggenheim Museum - which spirals upwards over three floors like an open snail shell. In the middle of the staircase is the sculpture "The more the better", created by Paik Nam-jun in 1988. Shortly after its inauguration in 1986, this pyramid consisting of 1003 television screens was erected in the museum. The media tower is a flickering monster whose psychedelic short films could quickly give the inclined viewer a headache. Even back then, this pyramid was considered the masterpiece of the "father of video art". When I stood in front of it again a good seventeen years later, the screens were black, the sound and the electrical crackling of

Braun's tubes had gone silent. Dead as a stuffed dinosaur, the 1003 screens now towered high into the air, no sound, no picture, just electronic waste in one place. Is there a better image for the short life of POP art or even the short life of media and fashions? The explanation for the standstill, the inoperability of the sculpture was quite simple. It was due to technical developments that defective televisions in this sculpture could no longer be repaired; spare parts were lacking and technicians were overwhelmed by the outdated technology. A sculpture that was barely twenty years old and paid homage to technology thus became a vanity symbol par excellence.

The real highlight, however, was meeting Kim Seo-kyung and Kim Un-seong. I had first met these two warm and talented artists in Regensburg and then saw them again in Hamburg. Both times, however, only briefly and always involved in representative activities. Now we were together for several hours in a confined space. In the museum, I immediately used the time to ask about personal role models, about artists that both of them see as an inspiration for their work, in whose nimbus they find themselves. To my surprise, the name of Käthe Kollwitz immediately came up. And then you led me to a wall on the second floor of the museum dedicated to the artists of Minjung Art. In view of the powerful visual language that I was able to perceive there, I immediately understood the connection and bow to Käthe Kollwitz.

After a good two hours, we finished our visit to the museum and set off to cover the 20 kilometers to the center of Seoul by car. Another two hours later, we arrived at the hotel. The volume of traffic around and in Seoul was so high on this Saturday evening - as it is almost every evening - that we only made progress at a snail's pace. Fortunately, our mood was not dampened by the cramped interior of the car - I was allowed to sit in the front as a passenger - or by the endless traffic jams. More or less trusting and following the navigation system, we arrived at our destination, checked into the Hotel Shilla Stay Gwanghwamun and met up at a nearby restaurant whose specialty was kalbi, i.e. pork belly cooked on a grill. The food was deliciously rustic and tasty. We continued to have a lot of fun together and I learned to appreciate I.'s translation skills more and more. As we said goodbye, I asked her openly if she could join us the next day, on Sunday, because at least I would be happy, it would take the pressure off Nuna and maybe she would learn something at the "House of Sharing". I. didn't want to commit herself, and she was also put off by the early time that had been set for Nuna's departure. So we left this point open. The farewell from Kim Seo-kyung and Kim Un-seong was also warm. As I assumed that we would see each other again and again, I waved to them without melancholy, but with great gratitude.
A short walk around the hotel block was to round off the events of this travel day, I memorized various high-rise silhouettes and marched off. A row of streets with brightly lit stores, stores and restaurants caught my attention, but the noise and

crowds of people put me off. Instead, I saw a small, traditional temple. I decided to meditate a little in the tranquillity of the temple complex and reflect on the day. To shorten the walk, I climbed over a low balustrade and realized that I had triggered an alarm by climbing over it. A siren blared, a cone of light bathed me in glaring light and security guards were standing right in front of me. When I realized the mishap I had committed, I dug out my existing Korean, which wasn't much, and tried to make it clear with my hands and feet that I had not acted with malicious intent, but merely out of curiosity. I immediately wanted to climb back over the wall. The guard seemed to understand me, but prevented me from climbing again. He opened a low gate and pushed me out of the temple grounds. Now, one experience richer, I directed my steps back to the hotel, which I found immediately without any problems. My room was on the fourteenth floor with an impressive view of the lights of the metropolis, some distance away newly built, modern high-rise buildings, but directly below me, on the opposite side of the street, several old, low houses, almost barracks; what an exciting interplay of old and new, so close together.

The next morning began with a meeting in a nearby South American-style coffee house. And not only my former school friend, U., but also Nuna and, much to my delight, Nuna's friend and her daughter turned up. Unfortunately, I had to hear that both mother and daughter were currently at loggerheads and not speaking to each other. My hope was that a change would be brought about during the course of the day. So the day began with a good, strong coffee and an unavoidable sweet. As we left the coffee house, I wondered about the large sculpture painted in pop colors opposite the entrance, a thin man, a good 5 meters tall, with a long stride, staring at the display of his laptop, which he carries in his left hand in front of him. He seems to be flying forwards, the horizontally waving scarf around his neck reinforcing this dynamic movement.

We got into our school friend's car and drove to the "House of Sharing". We had about a 90-minute drive ahead of us. The streets of Seoul, at around nine o'clock on a Sunday morning, were decidedly empty compared to the traffic jam of the previous evening. We drove east on the south side of the megacity, passing the "Needle", the tallest skyscraper in Korea. We quickly left the confines of the metropolis behind us and drove into the countryside, where it became quieter and quieter around us and the landscape was slightly hilly. Finally, we reached today's destination: House of Sharing. A facility to commemorate the fate of Korean women abducted by the Japanese military during World War II and forced into sex slavery. The facility consisted of several centers, the information center, a retirement home with a hospice section, a cemetery, a prayer hall with a museum. The stairs of the entrance area led through a gate-like opening to the first inner courtyard. This provides space for several portrait busts of deceased activists who once publicly acknowledged their history and fate and lived here at the center for a longer or shorter period of time. The busts resemble portraits, with inscriptions providing further information. Behind and in the last row of this collection stands what is probably the first bronze sculpture created on the theme of "comfort women". She stands upright, a young girl with a vacant gaze, dressed in the traditional han-bok. Her hair is braided into a tight ponytail on her back. A single flower grows out of the round plinth between her feet. A single blossom that is yet to bloom, just like the girl herself. The sculpture was created in 1997 from the painting "Unblossomed flower" into a three-dimensional sculpture. Her painted model was created by grandmother Kim Soon-duk, who was one of the best-known activists who publicized her fate as a "comfort woman" and appeared in public, especially at the weekly Wednesday demonstrations in front of the Japanese embassy in Seoul. A small-format model of the sculpture, painted in polychrome, stands in the museum, just as touching.

The tour of the information center, led by a specialist, was like a test of self-control and was extremely emotional. The suffering of so many hundreds of thousands of girls and young women was brought to life in this actually very small documentation center with a few original objects, a few replicas and many figures and texts. I was most impressed by two rather small objects which, after seeing them, left me in no doubt about the truth of the fates of the so-called comfort women, if I ever had any doubts. The two original objects were: A banknote, so-called "ghetto money" and an unused condom, both from around 1944.

The enclosed information about the banknote stated that the young women in the military brothels were paid with ghetto money. A service paid for with a currency that was only valid in a limited area, the ghetto, automatically stigmatized the owner and gave them no freedom. The misconception that Korean women entered into this dependency and lack of freedom of their own free will - as presented by the Japanese government - is incomprehensible. And on to the condom. The vernacular is disarmingly honest in many respects. For example, the information text on the condom explained that the Japanese soldiers referred to their condoms as "killing by first strike". In other words, they referred to the sexual assault of women and girls as the first killing tool, similar to a bayonet, a machete or a rifle. In one part of the museum, the lifelines of selected women were traced on world maps. This gave the viewer an insight into the women's abduction routes. Far away from their own homeland, they were deported by ship and rail to Indonesia, China and Thailand. After the war, after liberation, many of them nevertheless found their way back to their old homeland. I asked myself how a young person who was kidnapped and abducted from a village in a certain province at the age of 16, for example, and taken to a country six hours away by plane, how could a young person - from a country where a language other than his mother tongue was spoken - find his way back home after suffering and enduring terrible sexual, psychological and physical humiliation? The lifelines documented in the museum proved that a return was possible.

After walking through the two-story information center and museum, we were given the opportunity to visit and meet some of the grandmothers living here in person. This trip to the hospice was not easy, as we came into contact with people who were nearing the end of their lives, who were already demented and confused, some bedridden. Grandmother A. sat in the visitors' anteroom and greeted us cheerfully. She was used to up to one hundred people coming to see her and the other grandmothers every day. She was used to visitors paying her their respects and being the center of attention. We sat down with her, gave her some presents and listened to her. She told us that she had fought in the war and had suffered a wound, directly on her temple, which she was able to show us. Then she seemed exhausted and tired, and after a short pause she began to tell us again that she had fought in the war. We went on and visited Grandmother C. in her room. She was sitting on her bed with the television on. She apologized for not being able to get up to greet us, but Nuna found the right words, she praised grandmother and had a long conversation with her, guided by the many memorabilia in grandmother's small room. Another visit took us to Grandmother K., who was bedridden, but I had to stop here. Together with the school friend, we sat down in the waiting area of the hospice and tried to process the current perceptions through a simple and casual conversation. Finally, Nuna and her friend and daughter rejoined us. We said goodbye to the many friendly staff at the center who were always ready to help.

The rest of the way led us to a specialty restaurant, where the waiters prepared freshly caught young eel for us on the table grill over charcoal. A real treat for the palate and a welcome distraction.

We went back to Seoul by car. We wanted to visit the "Girl Statue for Peace", which had been standing in the center of the city in the immediate vicinity of the Japanese embassy since December 14, 2011.

Nuna and her school friend weren't quite sure where exactly the statue was located, so they both repeatedly asked young police officers who were patrolling the streets in small groups and standing at the entrances to houses, which was a clear indication that we were near an embassy building. We followed the signs and found ourselves standing in front of the "Girl Statue for Peace". I was a little startled because the statue was not really visible, it seemed rather hidden and completely atypical in its placement. While all, really all other sculptures in Seoul's public space stand on a raised place, at least on a pedestal, i.e. elevated and also visible to passers-by from a distance, the "Girl Statue" is literally parked at sidewalk level on the sidewalk wheel of the pedestrian path. It is only possible to see the statue when standing in the immediate vicinity. In addition, a low multi-person tent was pitched directly to the left of the sculpture. The tent cover was transparent, so you could look inside and see four young people who, I was told, were on twenty-four-hour guard duty. A guard whose mere presence ensured that there would be no attacks on the sculpture. However, the tent, which had the same ridge height as the top of the statue of the girl, completely obscured the view of the sculpture when approaching from the north; coming from the south, the tent foil distracted the view from the sculpture and one thought one was looking at a pile of garbage rather than approaching an important sculpture. In front of the statue of the girl were small bronze plaques on the bordering kerbs. Behind the statue, yellow butterflies were glued to the low enclosure wall of the adjacent tower block. And to the right of the statue of the girl was a uniformed policeman standing guard. To protect the statue? His function was not entirely clear to me, because when I wanted to sit down on the empty bronze chair for a documentary photo, he held me back with words and a light touch on the shoulder.

As a result, we only took photos that showed us behind the sculpture. We therefore had the same view as the statue and looked at the opposite side of the road, where two police crew buses were parked, with their engines running, probably 24 hours a day, seven days a week, ready to pick up police officers and drive off at any time. The exhaust fumes were discharged into the sewage system with hoses attached to the exhausts. Behind the team buses was another five-metre-high whitewashed wall that blocked the view of the property behind it, with a mesh fence topped with barbed wire in front of it.

Until a few years ago, the Japanese embassy building stood on this enclosed site.

The "girl statue" sat so small and inconspicuous opposite the embassy that I was forced to make a comparison with the Spanish hero Don Quixote. Just as Don Quixote fought against sacks of flour, lions in cages and, of course, windmills, the unwavering "Suri", a firm believer in truth and equality, who stands up for her values, for justice, just by being, by sitting quietly, no: sitting!

During the thirty minutes or so that we spent at the statue of the girl, passers-by who had deliberately made their way there kept coming. They took photos, some touched the bronze, some laid flowers. As we were leaving, I looked around again in the immediate and wider surroundings and suddenly had to laugh out loud, which visibly irritated some passers-by, Nuna, Mr. Park and the policeman. At a distance of perhaps two hundred meters, I recognized the polychrome sculpture of the rushed laptop carrier that had already attracted my attention that morning. I asked Nuna and Mr. Park, pointing in the direction of the statue, if that wasn't the coffee house where we had started the day a few hours ago, and why we hadn't visited the statue of the girl in the morning? Both were visibly uncomfortable with this discovery, but it showed how inconspicuously the statue is placed for those who have to look for it. For those who know the place, however, the site was and is outstanding and of symbolically high quality.

As it was getting darker and darker, we broke off this first visit and went to one of the many restaurants in the nearby, formerly very famous artists' and tourist district of Insadong. There we found a quiet restaurant in the basement and ended the day with dinner. Nuna and Mr. Park took me to the hotel, as Mr. Park´s car was parked in the underground garage. Once in my room, I sat at the window for a long time and looked out at the city lights, which was more calming and exciting than the many channels on the TV. Tomorrow we were to visit the Foreigner Cemetery and Franz Eckert's grave, which was to be a reunion with a project that I started in 1998 and completed in 2003. I also had an interview with a newspaper reporter coming up.

After skipping breakfast, I used the next morning to take a very early walk through the surrounding area and to the former royal palace, the Gyeongbokgung, whose name means "radiant bliss". The weather was fantastic, the sky bright blue and after a few minutes' walk I was standing between the statue of General Yi Sun-sin - the Korean naval admiral played a key role in fending off Japanese invasion attempts at the end of the sixteenth century - the building that housed the Japanese embassy and the Royal Palace. I was magnetically drawn to the architecture of the palace. According to my knowledge of feng shui theory, the way it is embedded in the surrounding and backdrop landscape alone is a great success. From inside the palace, the mountain range of the resting tiger can be seen on the right, the reclining dragon on the left, a high mountain cone, the watchful tortoise, is enthroned protectively in the background; in front is an open space, then the Ming Tang. In front of the main gate, a water dragon on the left and right protect the palace from the dangers of the water sources in the distant mountains. And a little further in front of the gate is the protective phoenix. All the elements are arranged in perfect harmony. This royal palace from the time of the Joson dynasty, completed around 1395 AD, is an excellent example of exceptional architecture that was planned, built and implemented according to the principles of feng shui. Its high energetic quality still has an effect today. At least that's how I felt about this place. And probably also all the thousands of visitors who flock to and from the Royal Palace every day.

But then it was already time to leave the place and go to the meeting point for the interview. In the neutral atmosphere of a café, Nuna and I met Mr. C. The conversation that followed was calm and matter-of-fact. Nuna translated very conscientiously, asking questions of both Mr. C and myself, so that I had the impression that the newspaper journalist understood the essence of our visit. After a good two hours, we said goodbye, of course not without taking a few photos in front of and with the "girl statue". The result of this meeting was published the next morning in the print version of the newspaper Jewon and simultaneously in the online version. The version translated into German can be found in the appendix.

Nuna and I now wondered what was behind the white wall that the "girl statue" was facing. Unfortunately, we tried unsuccessfully to get into some of the neighboring high-rise buildings to catch a glimpse of the supposed construction pit from the height of perhaps the thirteenth or fifteenth floor. However, as the people we approached neither wanted to understand our request nor to help us, we abandoned this attempt after a while, disappointed.

We took the S-Bahn to the Foreigner Cemetery. My aim there was to see the gravestone of the imperial court musician Franz Eckert. On my first visit to this cemetery, I was looking for historical connections between Germany and Korea, which I could establish through individual biographies. During this research, I came across Franz Eckert. Born in the German Empire in 1852, he worked his way up to become a military bandmaster and can be seen as the pioneer who first brought Western music, Western notation and Western musical instruments to Japan and then to the Korean court. He composed the first Japanese national anthem and later the first Korean national anthem. He lived in Korea until his death in 1916. His gravestone was damaged during the fratricidal war and when I stood in front of this damaged gravestone for the first time in 1998, I decided to have it restored. When I returned to Germany, I found my friend Axel Richter, a sculptor and supporter, who produced a bronze portrait plaque of Eckert. During my next visit in 2003, I presented this plaque to the then ambassador of the Federal Republic of Germany, who assured me that he would see to it that it was installed. Years later, I received a photo from a Korean friend that actually showed the restored stele with the portrait medallion. Today, however, I was finally able to see for myself that my little project was complete. I formed a ring with my visit. A ring closure that gave me a further idea in conversation with Nuna: We should start a traveling campaign. We should visit every statue, every monument that was erected in memory and as a reminder of the suffering of the so-called comfort women in the Asia-Pacific region as part of a world tour. In this way, a common thread would be laid across the globe, connecting all these places through our actions. This trip would have to be financed through ground-funding and the entire campaign would have to be transported in the social network in parallel, i.e. at the same time.

As we couldn't do anything else at the cemetery apart from taking one or two photos, we drove back into the city center to have a late lunch and finally a coffee. To round off this, my last day in Seoul - the next morning I was already heading back home to Frankfurt - I said goodbye to Nuna and strolled aimlessly through the adjacent streets, popping into various stores, especially the formerly famous Insa-dong, which offered me a rich variety of purely tourist stores, but also smaller art galleries and restaurants. Time passed quickly, darkness fell and I went to my hotel room. Again I sat by the window for a long time, finally packed my suitcase and spent my last night in Seoul.

To my great surprise, Nuna was waiting for me at the hotel reception the next morning. Although we had found out the exact location of the bus stop the day before, the express bus that was to take me from the hotel to the airport, her Korean side forbade me to go to the airport alone. She ended up taking me to the security checkpoints. In addition to the pleasant company, her presence had the great advantage that we were able to buy the daily edition of the Jewon newspaper in a newspaper kiosk and find our article there. Nuna skimmed the pages and smiled with satisfaction. Now she could let me board the A380 to Frankfurt with peace of mind.

Review and outlook

Back in my home country, I see myself confirmed in the explosiveness and urgency of the "Girls' Statue for Peace" project. Of course, this is just one project among many, but we cannot divide ourselves, but we can use our strength where we can achieve something. The issue of forced labor, prostitution in general, human trafficking, warfare, kidnapping, genital mutilation, terror, pollution, loneliness ... there are so many areas where we should and must take action. But with the help of the "girl statue" project, at least one topic is explicitly addressed as a pars pro toto. And by perceiving and accepting it, sensitivity can be triggered in the viewers, which initially revolves around the specific and found subject area. Once sensitized, however, the viewers and those touched will no longer be able to pass by other themes, problems and crises of this world, of this humanity, indifferently. Once touched, the desire to change, to improve, to do something will be set as a seed. The members of Punggyeong e.V. in Germany follow the call to want to bring about change and use the statue to attract attention, growth and change. The fact that this campaign was joined by other supporters, who actively and with their voices contributed to the "girl statue" coming from the USA to Hamburg, where it was set up in the Dorothee-Sölle-Haus for six weeks, then moved on to Frankfurt/Main, where it stood in the foyer of the Haus am Dom for several weeks in 2019 and then - as a project of the ASTA - was set up on the campus of Johann Wolfgang Goethe University in 2020, is great and deserves respect and gratitude. We can be very curious to see where the next stops of the "Girl Statue" will be. I am grateful that I was able to accompany the "Girl Statue" for a while; she will always have a place in my heart.

It remains to be hoped that the "Girls' Statue for Peace" will be allowed to stand again and again in the most diverse places in our Federal Republic of Germany and will inspire people of the most diverse backgrounds to engage in joint discussions and their own inner reflection. I am delighted to have been a small piece in the mosaic of this project. The stimulating contacts with interested and interesting people that I have been able to experience over the past three years have prompted me to write down this project description. My aim was to give a very personal and individual view of and into a project. If you would like to gain a much deeper insight into the issues involved, please consult the list of further reading in the appendix or visit the places I have mentioned.

The story continues! To be continued...

Appendix

626th material: Newspaper article in Jewon, November 12, 2018
We are contacting various institutes to set up the peace booths next year Dr. Martin Schmidt-Magin, Artistic Director of the German non-profit association Punggyeong Weltkulturen e.V.

"I would like to look at the sculpture from the top of a high-rise building. Do you have any ideas?" The German approached me with these words when we met in a café near the Japanese embassy on the morning of November 12. He is the artistic director of the German non-profit association Punggyeong Weltkulturen, which was founded last year. The association was supposed to set up the peace statue (Girl Statue for Peace) in the Bonn Women's Museum last August, but this did not happen. The Women's Museum, which originally promised to install the statue, hesitated to realize the project. It cannot be ruled out that pressure from the Japanese government played a role in this change of attitude.

The peace statue, which was to be erected properly in Bonn, was exhibited in the Dorothee-Sölle-Haus in Hamburg for six weeks from August 14 as an interim solution. He did not want to reveal where this statue is at the moment. He was invited by the Japanese Consulate General in Hamburg during the exhibition and was told that the Japanese government rejects any form of erection of a peace statue in Germany that commemorates the sex slave system of the

Japanese army during the Second World War.

What might the role of the artistic director at the Punggyeong Association be?
"I look for a suitable location for the statue. I contact a number of institutes throughout Germany and present our project." Schmidt-Magin, who experienced the failure of the peace statue, says: "I realized that we need reliable partners who can withstand all external resistance." When asked when the peace statue could be expected to be erected, he simply replied "Hopefully in 2019". When asked what the biggest challenge was, the answer was: "It's the intervention from the Japanese government."

He is also interested in the aesthetic value of sculpture. He plans to study the aesthetics of the statue in more detail and publish a monograph on the subject. On Saturday the 10th, he met the artist couple Kim Seo Kyung and Kim Eun Sung at the Korean National Museum of Modern Art in Gwacheon and talked to them for about two hours. How did he rate the peace jams artistically? "Aesthetically, the value is very high. The form is naturalistic, but at the same time it is at a high level of abstraction. There are no exaggerated gestures. No tragic or dramatic elements either. It reminds me of the serenity of the Buddhist Maitreya Bodhisattva (Korean National Treasure No. 83)."

The art historian completed his doctorate in art history at the Free University of Berlin. His doctoral thesis dealt with the artistic dispute between Goethe and the sculptor Gottfried Schadow on the question of what is the essence of art. He has been involved in the art trade since 1995. He has worked on the Frankfurt art auction market and is now a freelance art consultant, art dealer and exhibition curator. He works intensively with around 20 international artists.

Since 2004, he has published an independent series "REGARDEUR". Nine books have been published so far, including books about Yun Yi Sang, Lee Miruk and the Goethe Monument in Chicago. The tenth book will probably be about the Girl Statue for Peace (Peace Statue).

What conversation did he have with the artist couple? "I wondered what artistic role models they have and what artistic movement they are in Korean art history. By talking to them, I learned that they are from the Minjung art scene and clearly differentiate themselves from the playful and commercial works that are everywhere in the city. They are also very intellectual."

On Sunday the 11th, he also visited "The House of Sharing" and spent several hours there. "By visiting the House of Sharing, I was able to deepen my knowledge of history." He continued. "There I saw the military currency that was only valid in the camp. This meant that the victims of the system had no freedom outside. There was complete lack of freedom. I also saw condoms with <Storm No. 1> written on them. Sex was linked to homicide."

The last time the art historian was in Korea was 20 years ago. He saw the first statue of a girl for peace in front of the Japanese embassy in Seoul for the first time during this visit. "I would have been happier if the girl was in a spacious public space like in Suwon. But here the statue is at the edge of the sidewalk, so passersby might overlook it. I would be happier if the peace statue was placed in harmony with the surroundings or on a pedestal. "

As an art historian, he focuses on the topic of migration. Not only migrants in Germany, but also Germans who have moved to other countries arouse his interest. This led him to research the German composer Franz Eckert, who composed Gimigayo, the Japanese national anthem during the imperialist era, as well as the Korean national anthem of the defunct Korean Empire. Chinese painters living in Germany and Turkish buildings in Germany are also his areas of interest.

When did he become interested in the peace statue?

"In a gallery, I met Eun Hi Yi, the chairwoman of Punggyeong Today, and we talked about Lee Eungno. After some time, I learned about the history of the peace statue. Through the Eckert research, I already knew that the relationship between Korea and Japan was sensitive." He added: "My country's past also sparked my interest in the peace statue. "We have the problem of coming to terms with the Nazi era. Coming to terms with war crimes committed by Nazi Germany in the past is our task. That's why I also look at how other countries deal with it.

He believes that "there is no peaceful future if you don't look properly at the past." What does Germany's past look like? "Fortunately, we are objectively investigating war crimes in many research institutes. Citizens are aware of the crimes committed by Nazi Germany during the Second World War. Germans can also place the Holocaust memorial in the middle of the capital ",

He said the following about some radical right-wing movements that are trying to turn back the clock of history.
"Any democratic society we live in can speak for itself. A democratic society should be able to put up with the crazy thoughts of some people."

He also has a meditation teacher certificate. "In today's world, meditation allows us to find peace and gives us the opportunity to better understand people and art."

Further reading (international resolutions, chronological order)

30.07.2007 US-Congress-Resolution-121
H.Res.121 - A resolution expressing the sense of the House of Representatives that the Government of

Japan should formally acknowledge, apologize, and accept historical responsibility in a clear and unequivocal manner for its Imperial Armed Forces' coercion of young women into sexual slavery, known to the world as "comfort women", during its colonial and wartime occupation of Asia and the Pacific Islands from the 1930s through the duration of World War II.
12.12.2007 Resolution of the European Parliament on the so-called comfort women

24.07.2017 HUMAN RIGHTS COMMITTEE
NGO Alternative Report for LOIPR on the 7th Periodic Report of Japan Related Article: Article 8 (Elimination of slavery and servitude). JAPAN On Japan's Military Sexual Slavery Issue. Women's Active Museum on War and Peace (WAM)
30.08.2018 UNO CERD 2018 C JPN CO 10-11 32238 E

Epilogue

For some it is the "girl statue for peace" for others the "war girl". It is sad to see how opinions are so divided over one and the same work of art. And it is not only the Japanese government and Japanese citizens who are against the sculpture.
With this description of my journey with the bronze sculpture, I would like to provide a text that enables readers and viewers to gain a deeper understanding of the circumstances that led to the production of the statue and that accompanied the attempts to install the bronze in public spaces.

It was only three years that I was allowed to accompany the "Girls' Statue for Peace", but they were intense. And I can promise one thing: It will continue! To be continued ...

For your thoughts and notes:

bernd stöver geschichte des k
(1) Sexuelle Gewalt im Krieg
https://www.youtube.c
News
Infos
Aktuelles Projekt
Künstlernachlässe
YouTube
Suchen
Mädchenstatue für den Frieden
14.048 Aufrufe

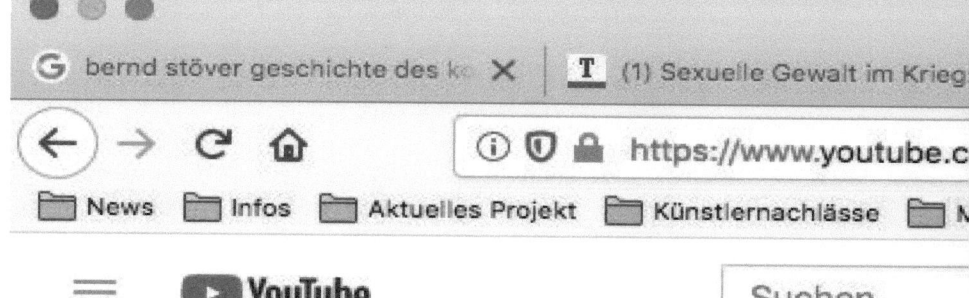

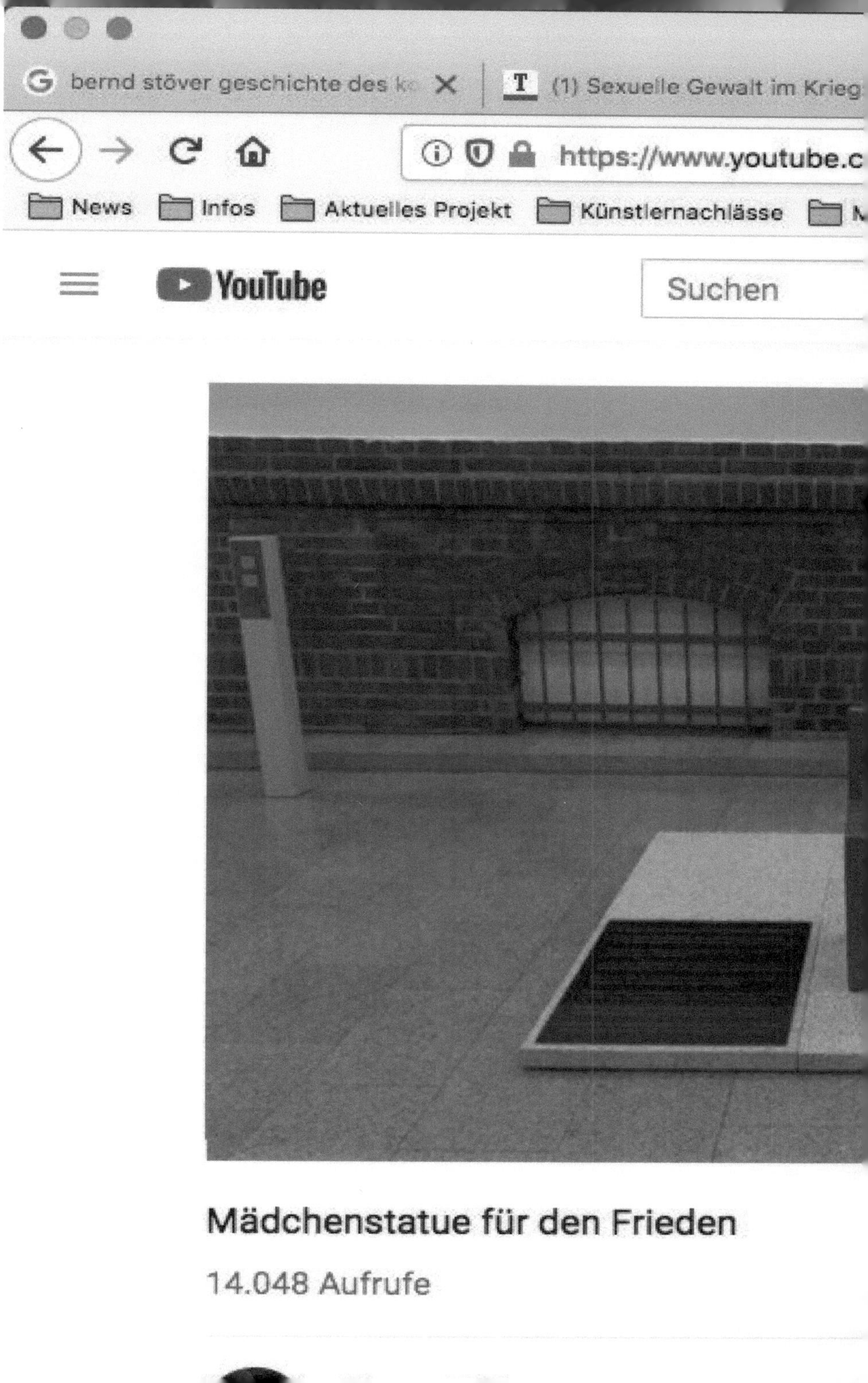

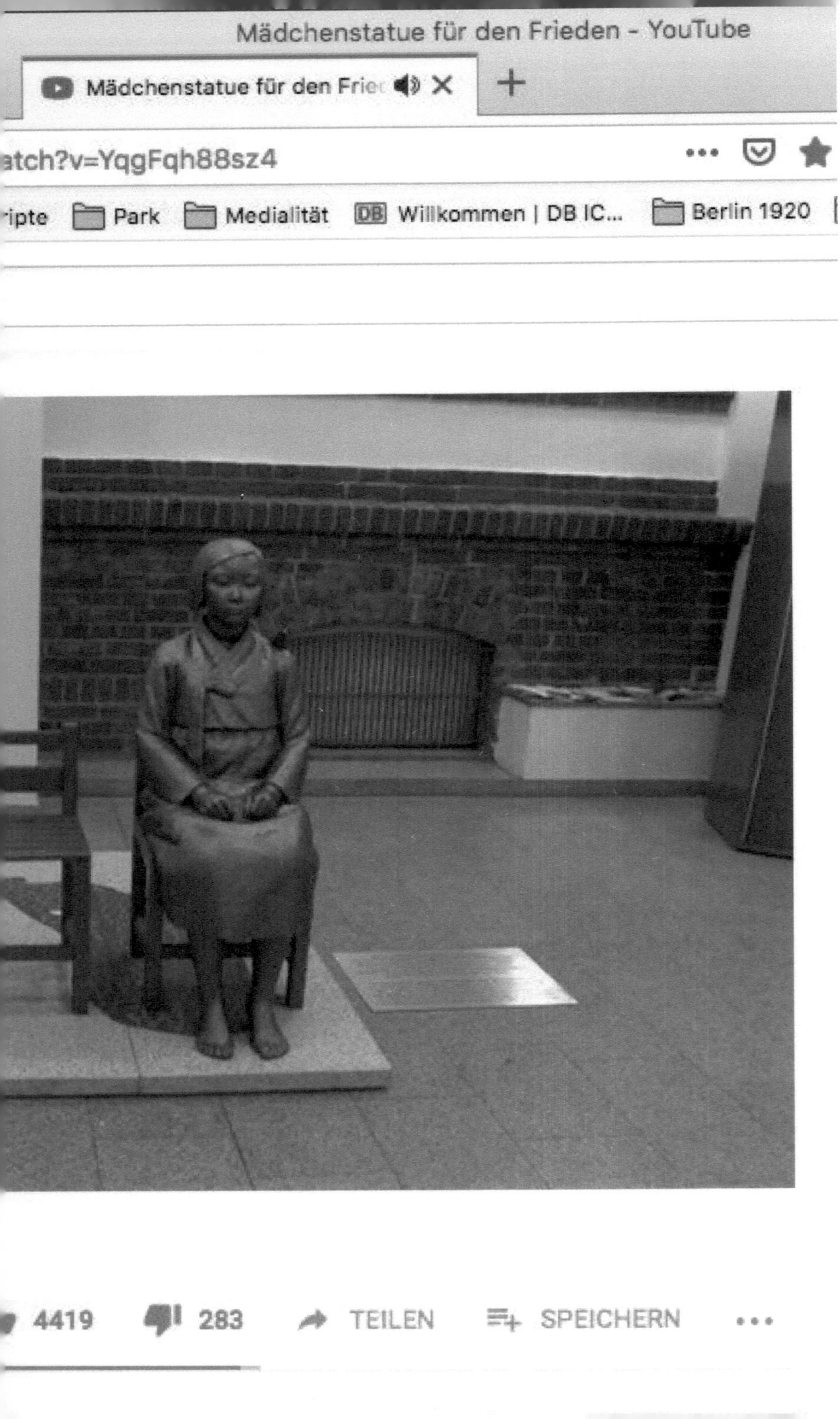
Mädchenstatue für den Frieden - YouTube
Mädchenstatue für den Frie
+
atch?v=YqgFqh88sz4
ipte
Park
Medialität
DB
Willkommen | DB IC...
Berlin 1920
4419
283
TEILEN
SPEICHERN

Diese „Mädchenstatue"
erinnert an das Leid brav...

남긴 '평화의 소녀상'은
어머니 언니 누나 동생입니다.
건네는 모든 이에게 사랑을 일깨워주고
평화를 노래하는 소녀상이기를 기원합니다.
– 대구대학교 총학생회 –

"내년엔 소녀상 세우려 독일 여러 접촉중이죠"

풍경
슈미트 예술감독

"평화의소녀상 주변 건물 높은 곳에서 소녀
상을 내려다보고 싶어요.방법이
없을까요."

12일오전서울 종로구의 주한 일본대사관
근처 카페에서 만난 독일인 마르틴 슈미트
(사진)가기자에게 건넨 말이다.그는 지난
말 독일에 평화의 소녀상을 세우려고 동포
와 현지인 10여명이함께만든 공익법인 풍
경(대표 이은희)의 예술감독이다.풍경은 지
난 8월소녀상을본 여성박물관에 세우려 했
으나 뜻을 이루다 못했다.애초 건립을 약속
한 박물관 쪽에서 유보적인 태도를
보여와
다.이런태도 변화엔 일본 정부의 압박이 영
향을미친것으로 보인다.

본에 영구히 자리할 예정이었던 소녀상
대신 8월14일부터6주동안함부르크 도로
테 췔레 하우스에서 전시됐다.지금 이 소녀
상이 어디에 있는지는 '대외비'이다.그는
전
시 기간에 주함부르크 일본 총영사관을 찾
아야 했다."총영사관에서보자고 해 갔더니
'일본정부는 어떤 형태의 소녀상도 독일에
건립되는 걸 반대한다'고 하더군요."

풍경 예술감독의 역할은?"소녀상이들어
설 적절한 장소를 찾는 것이죠.독일 전역엔
여러 기관과 접촉해 우리 프로젝트를 소개
하고 도움을 구하고 있어요."그는 소녀상의
8월건립이 무산되는 과정을 보면서 "정말
큰 부담이와도 흔들리지 않는 든든한
파트너가 필요하다는 걸확인했다"고
했다.
언제쯤 소녀상 건립이가능할까?"희망 연도

작년 동포·현지인 풍경 만들어
독일 내 소녀상 건립 추진
지난 8월 '본박물관'건립 무산
"최대걸림돌은 일본 정부 개입
**소녀상 예술성 주제로 책 낼
것"**

이주민 주제 관심 '미술사학자'

는 2019년입니다."가장큰어려움은? "일본
정부의 개입이죠."
그는 소녀상 조각의 미학적 위상에도 관
심이 많다.깊이 연구해 단행본으로 낼
계획
이다.지난 10일엔소녀상을 만든 김서경·김
운성 작가를 과천 현대미술관에서 만나 2시
간 이상 대화를 나누기도 했다.소녀상의 예
술성을 평한다면?"미학적으로 굉장히 수준
이 높아요.고도의 추상을 추구하면서도 인
간은 자연스러워요.또 과장된 제스처도
이지 않아요.비극적이거나 드라마틱한
요
도 배제했죠.금 동미륵보살반가사유
상
상의 고요함을 떠오르게 하죠."
그는 베를린자유대에서 미술사 연구로

가 고트프리트 샤도가 미
토론하는 내용을 박사 논문
다뤘어요."
1995년이후엔미술품 거래
랑크푸르트 미술경매회사
권 활동했습니다.거래·전
상을 매우 지금융하고싶어.
2004년부턴독립 출판물
(regardeur)시리즈'저술도
과 이미륵,시카고에 있는
등을
주제로 지금껏 9권을썼고
평화
소녀상 작가들과 어떤
작가들을다룰 계획이어
의 롤모델 그리고 작가들
름 속에 있는지가 궁금했
해
그들이 민중미술 작가이
곳곳에
흘러정었는1 우월래마움
작품을 머물렀다."나눔의 집
가를과 경계가 분명하다
되었고 매우 지적인작가
요."말을 이었다."거기서
통용된 돈인 군표를 보았
성노예
피해자들에게 자유가 없
증
거이죠.위안소는 완벽하
곳이

"당신이 틔운 참교육 씨, 이젠 후배들이

기관과

었어요. 돌격 1번(이치방)이라고적힌콘돔도 보았어요. 일본군이 섹스를 살인의 기술과 결합했다는 분명한 증거이죠."

이번이 1998년이후 20년만의한국 방문이란다. 일본대사관 앞 소녀상을 실물로 보기는

처음이다. "소녀상이 수원에서처럼 널찍한 공

공장소에 있었다면 더 기뻤을 겁니다. (대사관

앞 소녀상이)차도와 가까운 인도 위에 낮게

자리해 행인들이 지나칠 수도 있을 것 같아요.

술의 본질에 대해 소녀상이 주변 환경과 조화롭게 자리하거나

론에서 단상 위에 있다면 좋을 것 같아요."

│ 일을 해왔다. 프 미술사학도인그가 관심을 갖는 큰 주제는

·에서 일하기도 했 '이주민'이다. 독일내 이주민은 물론 다른 시 전문 컨설턴트 나

라로 간 독일 이주민에게도 마음이 끌린단다.

인 '리가르되르 일본 국가인 기미가요와 대한제국

:해왔다. 윤이상 애국가를

괴테 기림비 등을 만든 독일 작곡가 프란츠 에케르트를 10번째 책은 평화 연구한

것도 이런 이유에서다. 소녀상에 대한 대화를? "작가들 관심은

이 어떤 예술적 으 언제? "2002년쯤 한갤러리에서 이은회 대표

어요. 대화를 통해 를 만나 이응노 화백 이야기를 나누다 소녀상

고 대도시 곳곳에 얘기를 들었어요. 에케르트 연구를 하면서 상업적인 작품을 한

다는 걸 알게 되었 과 일본 사이에 걸린 문제가 민감하다는 걸 점도요."

집'을 찾아 몇시 잘 알고 있었어요." 자국의 지난 역사도 소녀

방문을 통해 역 상에 대한 관심을 키웠단다. "과거나치 독일

식을 얻게 되었어 일본 군대에서만이 저지른 전쟁범죄의 정리 문제가 늘

거요. 이는 성노예 리에

었다는 구체적 증 있어요. 그래서 다른 나라가 과거사 정리를

세 부자유한 곳이 어떻게 하는지 관심을 가지고 지켜봤죠."

sungman@hani.co.kr

그는 "과거를 제대로 들여다 보지 않고...

여현호 선임기자

'올,젠더와 법 연구소' 19일 설립

이사장 전효숙, 대표 전수안

사회·문화적 의미의 성별(젠더)관점에서 다양한 법 분야를 연구할 '사단법인올,젠더와 법 연구소'가 오는 19일 설립된다. 법무법인 원 주도로 만들어지는 연구소의 이사장에는 전효숙(왼쪽 사진)전 헌법재판관, 대표에는 전수안(오른쪽)전 대법관이 선임됐다. 연구소는 다양한 법 분야를 젠더와 관련된 시각으로 연구하고 연구 성과를 공유함으로써 젠더 관련 법과 실무를 발전시키고 평등한 사회를 실현하는 것을 목적으로 삼는다고 연구소 쪽은 밝혔다. 창립 기념으로 19일

오후 2시 서울 중구 을지로 페럼타워 페럼홀에서 이규 뉴욕시립대 교수를 초청해 '젠더

와 법,과제와 전망'콘퍼런스를 연다.

여현호 선임기자

성균관대 새 총장 신동렬 교수

성균관대는 제21대총장에 소프트웨어학과 신동렬(62·사진)교수가 선임됐다고 12일 밝혔다. 신교수는 1994년 성균관대 교수로 임용돼 정보통신대학장, 성균융합원장을 지냈다 임기는 내년 1월부터 4년이다.

인사

□ 국토교통부 <승진> □부이사관 <과장> □운영지원 전형필 □국토정책 김규철 □ 항공 □ 윤진환 □교

통정책조정 안석환

□ 문화체육관광부 <전보> □과장급 □문화예술교

선 과장 이용신 □교육부 파견 이정현

□ 교육부 □전남대 사무국장 박주용
□교원소청심

사위원회 심사과장 서기관

□ 신용보증기금 □상임이사 김동완

141

Regardeur X

Schriftenreihe für Kunst I Künstler I Betrachter

Regardeur – Schriftenreihe für Kunst | Künstler | Betrachter
Herausgegeben von Martin H Schmidt

Heft Nr. 1: Fritz Best-Cronberg – neu gesehen (2004)
Heft Nr. 2: Schaffenskraft Migration – Angelina Gradisnik (2007)
Heft Nr. 3: Franz Eckert – Li Mirok – Yun Isang. Botschafter fremder Kulturen.
Deutschland – Korea (2008)
Heft Nr. 4: Wilhelm Krieger – Tierbildhauer und Professor (2010)
Heft Nr. 5: Angelina Androvic Gradisnik – The Essential (2010)
Heft Nr. 6: Kunstguss in Lauchhammer – 1784 bis heute (2011)
Heft Nr. 7: Sun Wu Kung – Ein chinesisches Märchen in Deutschland (2012)
Heft Nr. 8: Das Goethe-Denkmal in Chicago (1914) – Made in Germany (2014)
Heft Nr. 9: Druckplatten expressionistischer Künstler aus dem Fritz Gurlitt-
Verlag (2016)
Heft Nr. 9a: Druckplatten expressionistischer Künstler aus dem Fritz Gurlitt-
Verlag. Ergänzungsband A (2017)
Heft Nr. 9b: Druckplatten expressionistischer Künstler aus dem Fritz Gurlitt-
Verlag. Ergänzungsband B (2017)
Heft Nr. 9c: Druckplatten expressionistischer Künstler aus dem Fritz Gurlitt-
Verlag. Ergänzungsband C (2018)
Heft Nr. 9 Sonderband: Das Buch Marathus (2019)

Dr. Schmidt Kunstberatung
Dr. Martin Schmidt-Magin
Am Gänsborn 10
61476 Kronberg/Ts.
Tel: 0163 361 25 18
eMail: info@curator4art.de
http://www.curator4art.de

Herausgeber: (V.i.S.d.P.) Dr. Martin Schmidt-Magin
1. Auflage: 2024

Gestaltung durch den Herausgeber
Herstellung und Verlag: Books on Demand GmbH, Norderstedt